How to Make People Like You

Learn to Improve Charisma, Build Rapport, Win Friends, and Connect Effortlessly

By: Devin White

ALL RIGHTS RESERVED

No part of this book may be reproduced, stored in a retrieval system, or transmitted in any form or by any means, electronic, mechanical, photocopying, recording, scanning, or otherwise, without the prior written permission of the publisher.

Limit of Liability/Disclaimer of Warranty: the publisher and the author make no representations or warranties with respect to the accuracy or completeness of the contents of this work and specifically disclaim all warranties, including without limitation warranties of fitness for a particular purpose. No warranty may be created or extended by sales or promotional materials. The advice and strategies contained herein may not be suitable for every situation. This work is sold with the understanding that the publisher is not engaged in rendering medical, legal or other professional advice or services. If professional assistance is required, the services of a competent professional person should be sought. Neither the publisher nor the author shall be liable for damages arising herefrom. The fact that an individual, organization or website is referred to in this work as a citation and/or potential source of further information does not mean that the author or the publisher endorses the information the individuals, organization or website may provide or recommendations they/it may make. Further, readers should be aware that websites listed on this work may have changed or disappeared between when this work was written and when it is read.

Table of Contents

Chapter 1: The Human Need for Connection 1

Chapter 2: What Is Likability? 13

Chapter 3: The Mindset of a Likable Person 21

Chapter 4: One Connection at a Time 39

Chapter 5: First Impressions: Welcome and Ease 47

Chapter 6: Body Language 71

Chapter 7: The Art of Conversation 83

Chapter 8: Make People Feel Important, Valued, and Respected 97

Chapter 9: Act Like a Friend 119

Chapter 10: The Likability Bias in Business 138

Chapter 11: Being You: Awesome, Likable You 149

Chapter 12: Putting It All Together 160

Likable, Wonderful You 164

Chapter 1: The Human Need for Connection

Introduction

"A human being is a part of the whole called by us [the] universe, a part limited in time and space. He experiences himself, his thoughts and feeling as something separated from the rest, a kind of optical delusion of his consciousness. This delusion is a kind of prison for us, restricting us to our personal desires and to affection for a few persons nearest to us. Our task must be to free ourselves from this prison by widening our circle of compassion to embrace all living creatures and the whole of nature in its beauty." ~ Albert Einstein

If you are feeling lonely, you are not the only one. It's ironic that we live in a world with over seven billion people, and yet so many feel the sting of loneliness.

In the West, we are lonelier than ever. We could blame it on a culture of busyness. We could blame it on the Internet and the false sense of connection we experience on social media. We could blame it on urban sprawl, where there is no town center that draws people together and people drive for an hour or more each way to their jobs. We could blame it on all of these factors, and more. But the fact remains, we are disconnected, and it is a problem.

We all want to be liked, appreciated, connected... and yet, becoming likable can be hard. It takes courage and it takes practice.

But I can promise you... when you are likable, people will approach you and doors will be opened to amazing professional and personal relationships.

If you commit to doing the work, your life will become richer, happier, more abundant, and easier.

I encourage you to read through this book several times. It contains a *lot* of information about becoming more likable.

The first read will give you an overview of what it means to be likable and it will build awareness of the traits that you possess and the ones that need developing.

The second read will help you fine-tune your approach. It will let you focus on the traits that need the most work.

As you go through the book, be sure to do the exercises at the end of each section. This is where the magic happens. You have to put them into practice if you are going to acquire the *skill* of likability.

That's right! Likability is a skill that we're all born with, but very quickly, we forget how to connect.

Why We Can't Connect

"Connections were what kept people tied to the world. Without connections, there was nothing left to stop them from simply floating away." ~ Eliza Maxwell

We desperately need connection, but many of us have forgotten how to connect. We don't live in tiny villages anymore; most of us live in huge, bustling, impersonal cities, or in suburbs where people live isolated lives in their apartments, emerging only to go shopping or to work.
This is for you, dear reader, if you feel lonely, like an outsider, unwanted and unloved.

We instinctively know that we want to belong... that we *need* to belong... and yet many of us don't know how to break through the barriers. And these barriers are self-imposed. Not on purpose, of course; nobody wants to be left out or disliked... but they are learned behaviors, nonetheless. We'll go more into that in a later chapter.

The good news is you can become a widely liked person, even if you've been a "nobody" your entire life.

Think about it: every baby born into the world is a happy, whole, content little being that just wants to be connected to everyone and love everyone. A baby holds no prejudices. A baby does not lack self-esteem. *A baby knows that a smile and a touch are everything.*

It's only our life experiences and conditioning that bring us to the point where we forget *how* to connect. We are introduced to prejudice ("You can't like them, they are *different*"). We are introduced to judgment ("He's so fat, he can't possibly be a good dancer"). We are introduced to negative comparisons ("She's much prettier than you, there's no way you can make friends that easily"). We are introduced to ego ("Wow, you beat your race record, that's nice; I ran that race too and found it a ridiculously easy course"). And so on.

Unlearning Unlikable Behaviors

"The most useful piece of learning for the uses of life is to unlearn what is untrue."
~ Antisthenes

Any unlikable behaviors you exhibit can be unlearned.
Most of how you see yourself, most of how you feel about yourself, is based on false perceptions of who you really are.

Over time, you "learn" about yourself from other people. Someone tells you that you are stupid, and you believe them because they are an authority figure. Someone attractive tells you that you are ugly. Someone who's jealous of you tells your friends you are actually a jerk.

Whoever came up with the children's rhyme, "Sticks and stones can break my bones, but words will never hurt me" was, no joke, an absolute idiot. Words *do* hurt, and they leave lasting scars that drive the way we see ourselves, and the way we interact with others—or avoid interacting as a way to avoid getting hurt.

In an attempt to not get hurt, to protect our fragile hearts, many of us learn unlikable behaviors. These coping mechanisms may have worked at the time of the hurt… but now, they are also making it hard for people to reach inside and say "hi."

As you read through this book you will recognize some unlikable behaviors in yourself. Please do not take them as judgment. Take them as guides to awareness of what needs fixing.

Just as you learned some unlikable behaviors, you can unlearn them. In this book you will learn to open your mind and heart to "others"; to release judgment; to look for things in common instead of differences; to drop the ego; to communicate effectively; and of course, you will learn the art of making the person you are with feel important, accepted, valued, and respected, which will be reflected in the way people treat you.

Again: read through the book, do the exercises, and then come back at least once more to fine-tune the process and work on the areas you are weakest in. Within a short time, you will become so likable that getting new friends and forging lifelong connections will become incredibly easy.

But first... why is it so important to be likable?

Why can't you just go through life as a loner or a curmudgeon? Well sure, you can get by. You can even become wildly successful. But you won't have the one thing that's necessary for a truly rich, fulfilling, happy, and content life: friends.

You can survive, but you can't thrive, without others.

It Takes a Village

"When it comes right down to it, whatever business you are in, you are in the people business. After all, people prefer to do business with people and companies they find likeable." ~ Karen Salmansohn

We all know people who effortlessly attract people and enjoy rich, meaningful, and deep connections. Others seem to be perpetually on the outskirts, never part of any "tribe." Then there's the third group, people who are often surrounded by people and appear to be socially engaged yet feel utterly alone.

Whichever group you belong to (and this can be fluid throughout your life), there's one thing that is either present or lacking that determines the group you belong to: likability.

Why Likability Matters

"If you're a likable person and you're passionate, then people are drawn to that wherever you are in the world." ~ Joe Wicks

Whatever you want to accomplish, most opportunities come through other people. People are more likely to give opportunities to the people they like.

You have to be liked before you can be loved. You have to be liked before you can be invited in. In any situation, people are more willing to help you if you are likable.

Everyone wants to be accepted into a group (and by this, I mean a psychologically healthy group of individuals who are supportive, positive, and respectful) and knowing what will make you accepted *for who you are* is vital to understanding the intention behind the exercises in this book.

What will get you accepted? It's not your looks, social connections, education, money, knowledge, skills, or talent. It's not conformism.

It's being likable.

Ultimately, this usually backfires. You can have the smoothest pickup lines or Jedi mind-trick closing skills. But if people don't like you, they are probably not going to say yes. If they don't like you, you will be seen (and treated) as an irritant instead of a welcome member of a group. If they don't like you, you won't inspire them. If they don't like you, you won't be invited.

It's interesting that many people don't prioritize likability. They would rather perfect their sales pitch, or learn how to persuade others, or basically focus on the tactics to get what they want, rather than become a likable person.

Of course, likability isn't just about sales, or business. It's about life. Even if you are a hardcore lone wolf who insists on doing everything solo, at some point you are going to need others to train you, educate you, equip you, or somehow support you, and that path is much easier if you are likable.

Yes. You *can* accomplish something spectacular all 100% on your own, with online resources, and never say a single word to someone and never ask for help.

But consider this: *what will that accomplishment really mean, if you can't share it with others*, especially those that helped you make it happen? The victory will be hollow.

Throughout your life, you need people. The basic question that we all ask ourselves when we meet someone—consciously or unconsciously—is, "Do I like this person?" (Do I want to do business with this person, become friends, enter a relationship, help this person, etc.?)

Two people may have equal skills, talents, and capabilities and therefore the same opportunity to excel. But do you actually want to spend hours every day with this person? The likable one will almost always achieve his or her goals faster.

If you feel (or have ever felt) unlikable, take heart. Likability is a skill, and you can develop it by following the steps in this book.

But first, let's define what likeability is not.

What Likability Is NOT

"I could see (though not as clearly as I do now) that one of my biggest problems was me. Because I wanted everyone to like me and to approve of me, I tried to be nice to everyone all the time and this proved a remarkably efficient way of losing control over my life." ~ John Cleese

Let's clear up some misconceptions about likability.

Unfortunately, likability has developed a bad reputation. Likability often gets confused with being weak, generic, and selling one's soul for the sake of being accepted. It can also be associated with con artists who use their charm to steal or swindle people out of money.

If you look deeper, though, the qualities often confused as likability really represent an *unlikable* person: the exact opposite of what we're trying to accomplish here.

Likability Is Not Being Likable All the Time

"Our biggest struggle as human beings is to project ourselves as something that society has deemed admirable or likable instead of being honest." ~ Matthew Shultz

Most people are not likable all the time. We all have bad days, and we all have days where we aren't especially nice. Parents aren't always likable, kids aren't always likable, spouses aren't always likable, even friends aren't always likable. We're humans, we're flawed. As long as we're kind most of the time, people can forgive our bad days.

Challenge

When someone you love or admire had a really bad day and showed a dark and ugly side of themselves, how did that alter your perception of them? Were you able to forgive them and keep on liking them? If the love or like is deep, then you probably did. And people will extend the same forgiveness to you when you are a likable person who's having a bad day and you are not being nice.

Likability Does Not Mean Being Perfect

"A likable character isn't one who does nothing wrong." ~ Alice Ripley

You may have noticed that likable movie or book characters are often the forgettable ones. Our focus is on the flawed characters, the villains, because they aren't afraid to show their dark side.

But in real life, we are all flawed. Nobody is perfect. In fact, perfectionists are often disliked because they take things too seriously. Perfectionists aren't much fun, in the grand scheme of things. We don't really want to hang out with them because they are obsessed with things being "just so." We don't want to support or help them because we feel judged that our efforts aren't good enough.

Challenge

If you are a perfectionist, try letting go and see how much easier it is to get along with others. Take note of their attitudes toward you. If you are not a perfectionist, observe what perfectionists do around people to try and control the situation. It's not very likable, is it?

Likability Does Not Mean Being a People-Pleaser

"If you find yourself craving approval, you are low on self-love. Stop grasping for a few scraps wherever you can. Go home and make yourself a feast. Love yourself deeply today." ~ Vironika Tugaleva

Being likable does not mean you have to agree with everyone else, or that everyone has to agree with you! It does not mean that you have to drop everything and do what someone asks.

Of course, we all want to be helpful and yes, sometimes helping out means putting ourselves last. But if it happens often, and if you find yourself becoming resentful, then you are saying yes for the wrong reasons.

People-pleasers give up who they are; they have no boundaries, and they try to mold themselves into someone they are not, thinking this will make people like them. It does not.

People walk all over people-pleasers, use you mercilessly for their own gains, disrespect you, and treat you badly: the exact opposite of how likable people are treated.

Even if you are getting something out of it (usually it is done for attention and validation) being a people-pleaser is an unlikable trait.

Likable people know how to say "no" without burning bridges. They have firm boundaries and uphold them. They don't try too hard. They don't put aside their own needs to do things for others and end up feeling resentful and exhausted. They never grovel in a desperate plea for attention.

Likability Does Not Mean Conformity or Becoming a Clone

"I don't try to be likeable. The worst thing people do is present versions of themselves to the world that aren't real." ~ Patrick Marber

Many people simply try too hard to be liked, and this usually backfires because in the process they try to be someone other than themselves. People who sacrifice who they are just to be liked aren't very likable, because they come across as inauthentic brown-nosers.

In an attempt to fit in and be liked, people often consciously or unconsciously adopt different fashions, different language, different speech mannerisms, and different behaviors to the point where they basically become clones of a person they admire or a group they want to belong to.

This is unfortunate because they still do not fit in. *What fits in is the mask they wear.*

Likability does not mean you should try to become someone else. It's a social skill that helps you connect with people.

Likable people are unique individuals and they embrace their individuality. They do not try to mimic everything their friends (or people they admire) say or do. They may mirror body language during conversation (a valuable skill), but they are also confident in their own style. They aren't afraid to dress differently or make different choices than their group.

Challenge

Notice people who conform to fit in. Maybe you know someone who completely changed just to be part of a group (maybe that person is you?). If it is people you observe conforming to fit in, do they look happy? Are they actually fully accepted by the group, or are they being laughed at behind their backs? If you did this (or do it now), how do you feel about being part of this group?

Likability Is Not the Same as Popularity

"Many people feel that if they're lonely, that means that they're not likable or that they're broken in some way." ~ Dr. Vivek Murthy

Although you might associate likability with popularity and being the center of attention, many likable people actually couldn't care less about winning popularity contests or being part of the "in" crowd. They often have a small, close-knit group of friends whom they treasure, but have no interest in surrounding themselves with groupies. Of course, many people who are popular are likable. Others are popular because they have gained a certain status and use their popularity to influence others; and their status and power do not automatically make them likable.

The real difference is that likable people tend to feel less loneliness than those whose power, celebrity, or status has attracted a following. Ultimately, being likable is far, far more important than being popular.

Challenge

Observe popular people. Take note of what makes them popular. Is it true likability (such as an ability to put people at ease, great storytelling, ability to make people laugh, including everyone, or being encouraging?), or is it their looks, last name, fame, fortune, or status? Is the person actually nice and likable, or are they self-centered prima donnas? The difference is easy to spot!

Observe people who are likable. These are the traits you will be developing in this book.

The next chapter discusses the qualities that make a person likable.

Chapter 2: What Is Likability?

The Truth About Being an Awesome Person

"It's nice to see a friendly face or have someone know your name." ~ Jillionaire

Likability is most often associated with being a "good person," but surprisingly, likability actually has very little to do with character. You could be heroic and likable, or you could be timid and likable. You could be dishonest and likable, or you could be honest and likable. There are plenty of "upstanding citizens" that are extremely unlikable, and plenty of dishonest, morally dubious people that are a lot of fun to be with and treat you with respect.

Someone could be a total con man and have the ability to charm anyone; or, someone could be considered important in their business or community and be almost universally despised.

Unfortunately, this means that some people can come across as likable and then turn around and do something awful.

But in general, being a good person does make you likable!

The point is, likability is a trait that anyone can develop, and it is in your best interest to do so because likable people generally win at this game we call life. They generally find it easier to get what they want and achieve their dreams.

So, what does it mean, exactly, to be likable?

As I mentioned, likability is a learned skill. Remember: you were born 100% likable and lovable! As with most of us, childhood conditioning and negative social experiences may have made it harder to connect with others and cause us to develop some unlikable characteristics. But again, don't worry. What can be learned, can also be unlearned.

When you understand the traits that make you likable and you develop those traits, you will automatically find it easier to make friends and foster deep and meaningful relationships.

Likeable people almost universally exhibit the following traits and behaviors:

1. They are nice (kind) to others. Being nice is another term that has gotten a bad reputation because it is sometimes associated with weakness. However, you can simply think of being "nice" as being kind. Likable people are always finding small ways to be extra kind, and this gets noticed.

2. They show genuine interest in other people. You might be surprised at how many seemingly confident people are actually very nervous and unsure of themselves in a social situation where they are meeting new people. But you will notice the ones that fit in easiest are the ones who display a genuine interest in others and tend to steer the conversation away from themselves. Encouraging people to talk about themselves builds rapport. They encourage others to share a personal story instead of going on and on endlessly about themselves.

3. They present an easygoing, positive, and optimistic attitude. Likable people aren't tense, stressed, uptight, or rigid about how things are "supposed to be." They don't get upset when things fail to go their way; rather, they go with the flow and shrug things off with a laugh. Even if they are not natural comedians, they can see the humor in a situation and lighten the mood. Their more lighthearted view of the world puts people at ease and helps diffuse tense situations.

4. They are empathetic. Likable people are keenly observant. They are attuned to others and avoid doing or saying things that offend or make life more difficult for others. They have a well-developed ability to put themselves into the other person's shoes. They are good listeners who can act as a sounding board, letting people talk things out and come to their own conclusions.

5. They have passions. Likable people are "on fire" about something (or several somethings). They visibly come alive when they are talking about what they love, but again, they are able to become excited about something that someone else loves. Ultimately this translates to an ability to support friends and family in going after their dreams, even if they are vastly different from yours (and who doesn't love people who support their dreams?).

6. They leave their ego at the door. Egotistical, self-centered people are almost universally unlikable. Likable people are focused on elevating others: for example, giving credit to their team, their coach, or even their parents as the real reason they won, not their athletic talents or brutal training. Successful likable people are not self-defeating in their speech, yet they are genuinely humble and very much aware that they didn't get to where they are without the help of others.

7. They are genuinely supportive. Likable people genuinely enjoy other people's successes and never express jealousy at someone's good fortune. They elevate others with genuine praise, they are generous with their help and wisdom, and they freely share credit. They do not give empty praise just to be liked; so when you are praised by a likable person, you know it is genuine.

8. They are good communicators. Likable people communicate clearly and are often good storytellers. You never have to guess what they are thinking. They are not blunt or rude but explain their thoughts in detail in a way that isn't critical. They encourage people to share thoughts and opinions. They listen deeply to ideas and other points of view (not half-listening while formulating a response). These traits make them very easy to talk to.

9. They are inclusive. Likable people don't form cliques. They make a conscious effort to include others; and therefore, likeable people are more likely to be included, as the people they bring into a group will reciprocate.

10. They share secrets… and keep them. Likable people use self-disclosure as a relationship-building technique. As part of a normal conversation, they don't probe deeply with personal questions (they don't interrogate); instead, they share increasingly intimate information about themselves, which creates a bond and encourages the other person to open up. Just as importantly, likable people faithfully keep secrets.

11. They are generous and helpful. Likable people operate out of generosity, with an attitude that there's enough for everyone and competition should be just for fun. They do not operate from a scarcity or lack mentality and would give you the shirt off their back if asked.

12. They are open-minded. Part of being interested in others is a genuine desire to understand someone's point of view. Likable people are open-minded and eager to learn. They never push their views on others. Rather, they are flexible and open to alternative perspectives, with an understanding that their way is not the only way.

13. They use friendly body language. Likable people consciously and unconsciously say "I like you, I am friendly, and I am not a threat" with their body language. They make eye contact (but don't give you a creepy, intense stare). They smile a genuine smile, not a fake social smile. They lean toward you in conversation. They mimic your body language.

14. They are self-aware. Likable people are aware of the impact of their words and actions on others and do their best to avoid hurting others. If they unintentionally hurt someone, they immediately apologize and make amends.

15. They allow themselves to be vulnerable. Emotional openness such as admitting flaws and weaknesses does not come naturally to many people because we fear that emotional exposure could mean rejection. However, likable people take this risk, especially when initiating or strengthening friendships. They are aware of their flaws and attributes, readily admit their weaknesses (rather than waiting for them to be revealed) but will not use them as excuses. They will admit they don't know everything and won't push their agenda because they are open to other ideas and approaches.

16. They ask for help when needed. Since likable people are not know-it-alls and readily admit that they don't know how to do something, they also understand the need for cooperation and so they ask for help. Many people shy away from asking for help because they don't want to be seen as helpless or as a burden. However, most people naturally like to help, and likable people know this. Asking for help invites interaction and connection—and makes the helper feel valued. However, this does not mean that likable people are helpless. They are helpers. They do what they can, and only ask for help when a situation or task is well outside of their abilities.

17. They do not offer unsolicited advice. As expert as likable people are, you won't find them butting in and giving unsolicited advice. They will offer advice when asked but their real skill lies in helping people solve their own problems by talking it out.

18. They see others how people want to be seen. It's natural for people to want others to see them in a certain light, in a way that is aligned with their beliefs about themselves. Likable people are good at pointing out people's attributes (in a genuine way).

19. They emphasize shared values. People are more attracted to people who are similar to them. This does not mean that likable people don't stay true to their beliefs; but they are able to put more emphasis on shared values rather than bringing attention to differences. Shifting the focus onto shared values is a way for any diverse group to bond.

20. They use physical touch. This varies by culture (as some cultures are more physical than others), but likable people are more apt to use casual touch. They use subliminal touch (they touch someone so subtly that the person hardly notices, such as touching their arm) to make people feel comfortable. A University of Mississippi and Rhodes College study focused on the effects of subtle touch on restaurant tipping. Waitresses were instructed to either briefly touch their customers hand or shoulder as they were returning their change, or not touch them at all. The waitresses who touched their customers earned significantly larger tips than those who did not.

21. They are valuable teammates. Because of their social skills, likable people are naturally cooperative in shared endeavors, often putting aside their egos for the common good.

22. They are natural leaders. Because people like them, they often end up in leadership positions. However, they may be just as content being part of the team in a supporting role. Leadership is another concept that is often misunderstood. It is *not* the act of forcing people to do your bidding. It is the act of bringing out the best in everyone to achieve a common goal: and nobody excels at this better than likable people. As leaders, likable people are not dictators or petty managers. Rather, they lead by example and use their interpersonal skills to foster team spirit and support people in not only doing their jobs but going above and beyond their duties.

23. They solicit opinions. Even in a situation where people have wildly opposing points of view, likable people will immediately put people at ease by respectfully soliciting their ideas and opinions. When people feel heard and valued, barriers come down and cooperation can begin.

24. They are present. Likable people are here, now, when they are with others. Being attentive to the person they are with means not thinking ahead to their grocery shopping, or back to that one time that guy said something stupid, or ahead to how they are going to introduce their sales pitch… the point is, they are fully present and engaged with the conversation, not lost in thought a million miles away.

25. They do not complain, judge, blame, or criticize. They are very aware that the words they say become part of how they are perceived, so their words—especially when speaking about others—are kind, respectful, positive, and compassionate. They never exhibit traits like jealousy, and do not engage in gossip.

26. They make people feel safe and comfortable. Likable people possess the ability to pull people out of their shell by asking open-ended questions and getting people talking about themselves, which immediately creates a bond.

This is a long list of traits that are essential for becoming a likable person. But if you take them on one by one, you will see that within a short time you will find it much easier to approach and befriend people.

This book will give you the step-by-step blueprint for developing or strengthening these traits in yourself. One step at a time, you will see that it is very doable to become a well-liked person!

Chapter 3: The Mindset of a Likable Person

Believe You Are Likable, and You Will Be!

"I know for sure that what we dwell on is who we become." ~ Oprah Winfrey

You are not being asked to make any sudden changes and immediately adopt all of the traits that make people likable.

However, in order for you to be a likable person, you have to think like one. You have to *be* likable in your mind first.

In this chapter we'll outline some proven ways to boost your self-image and confidence, so it becomes much easier to approach people and start conversations.

First, it is important to recognize that your mindset is what's really holding you back from making friends. Remember the baby, born with love for everyone, and an innate ability to connect? You can get back to that pure and wonderful state where you remove your barriers to connection.

Self-Talk: You Are What You Say You Are

"The mind is everything. What you think, you become." ~ attributed to Buddha

What you tell yourself repeatedly becomes a self-fulfilling prophecy! If you are constantly repeating statements like, "It's so hard to make friends," "People don't like me," "I'm too shy to say hello," or "I never know what to say," then you can be sure that you will start to behave as if these statements are true! Whether you say things like this out loud or to yourself, your words influence you very, very powerfully.

Over the years, you've probably repeated statements like this thousands of times, so it is no wonder they are a part of your "operating system": the way you see yourself and the way you believe you fit into the world.

Remember: nobody is born shy or socially awkward. These are learned behaviors based on what we hear as kids and our own experiences with rejection.

The bad news? Your beliefs about making friends are probably deeply ingrained.

The good news? Anything that is learned, can be unlearned.

Challenge

Write down the answers to the following self-awareness statements about how you see yourself as a friend:
- People like me: True or False
- I am a good friend: True or False
- It's easy for me to make friends: True or False
- I can start conversations with people easily: True or False

If you are like most people, your answers tend to lie somewhere in the middle: "It depends."

And that's okay.

Your first challenge is to upgrade the way you talk about yourself and friendship.

If you change your self-talk, you can literally talk yourself into being a likable person no matter the situation: whether you are within your comfort zone or way out of it.

This all-important chapter will give you the tools to upgrade the way you think, feel, and speak.
I'm not going to mislead you, however. Upgrading your mindset is an ongoing process that will require a lot of practice. But it will lay the foundation that will make the challenges easier; together, a mindset upgrade as well as practical exercises will do wonders!

Let's begin with a 30-day challenge that will give you some small wins very quickly, and eventually, a dramatic change in your outlook and self-talk.

The 30-Day Likability Mindset Challenge

"Whatever the mind can conceive and believe, it can achieve." ~ Napoleon Hill

Commit to 30 days of the following exercises and a whole new "you" will start to emerge.

Why is it important to commit to 30 days? That's about how long it takes to imprint a new habit, whether it is a physical habit or a thought habit. For best results, continue well past 30 days, but this is a good start to show you just how powerfully you have been talking yourself out of friendships, and how you can talk yourself into meeting amazing new friends.

The exercises only take about 5 minutes each, so it is not a big shakeup to your routine. The more relaxed you can be when doing the exercises, the better. Do these exercises first thing in the morning before your mind gets busy with the day ahead, and again last thing as you fall asleep so your mind can process the information as you sleep.

Here is the process:

1. Read through all of the exercises all the way through before starting so you know what to expect and so you fully understand the reasons behind this method.

2. Consistency is important. After all, repetition is how your current beliefs about yourself were imprinted. It's better to do a short session daily than to try to do more on a day "when you have more time" (we all know how that goes). Again, these are short exercises… tiny steps that will yield huge results.

3. Boost your success rate by practicing the exercises whenever you can throughout the day (while exercising, on your lunch break, while making dinner or doing chores). If you can't, don't worry; a quick morning and evening session will work!

The Visualization Exercise (Mental Rehearsal)

"Formulate and stamp indelibly on your mind a mental picture of yourself as succeeding. Hold this picture tenaciously and never permit it to fade. Your mind will seek to develop this picture!" ~ Dr. Norman Vincent Peale

What you think about, comes about. Have you heard this phrase? It does not mean simply sitting around thinking about something you want, and having it magically appear. It means that when you *see and feel* yourself in a particular state (for example, surrounded by wonderful friends); then your thoughts and actions will naturally align themselves with that mental image.

What you are doing in this visualization exercise is training yourself to imagine the best-case scenario instead of the worst. Right now, you are probably imagining how hard it is to make friends. You may be imagining how nervous you feel in social situations, or you are imagining being rejected.

The kind of visualization you are doing now isn't doing you any good. If you direct your imagination and put your focus on what can go perfectly right—easily making friends—then over time, you will create new neural pathways that make it easy and natural to imagine making friends. Your brain will become comfortable with it. And then, you will feel more at ease in social situations, it will be easier to walk up to someone and introduce yourself, you will know how to keep a conversation going, and you will be a natural at making people feel good.

Basically, in this exercise you are mentally rehearsing how great it feels to have more friends.

At first, this will feel strange and you may feel like you are lying to yourself. It's a lot like going to the gym: at first it hurts, and then you build muscle and the exercises get easier. Commit to this exercise, even if you feel it is weird, for 30 days and see what happens!

Elite athletes use mental rehearsal to reinforce their training and to help make their physical actions automatic when they are in competition. You want to get to this point too, where what you are doing in making friends is so second-nature that you don't doubt yourself anymore; you just do it.

Your brain cannot differentiate between what is "real" and what you imagine! That's why worry has such a hold on people: the situation they imagine going horribly wrong is so real that it triggers the stress response, even though the imagined scene lives only in the mind! Consciously introducing a best-case outcome feels much better. And it helps you take the steps necessary to gain new friends.

Challenge

Read through the steps and perform this exercise at least once and preferably several times, every day for 30 days.

1. **Get into a comfortable position, lying down or sitting.**

2. **Close your eyes and take a couple of very deep breaths to quiet your mind.**

3. **Imagine a scene where you are with a friend or surrounded by a group of friends.** You may feel more at ease imagining a scenario with just one other person, and that's fine. As you get comfortable with imagining yourself with one person, add another person until you are surrounded by a small group. Imagine people walking up and joining your group.

4. **Put yourself in this scene as if it is happening right now.** You aren't *meeting* new people. You are *already with* amazing people who are fun to be with. These people like you, they want to be with you, and you want to be with them. It's important that you are in the picture.

5. **Make it as real as you can.** Give your mind "visual evidence" of yourself surrounded by awesome people who really like you. What are you doing with your friend or

friends? Having drinks? Playing games? Listening to music? Going for a walk? Shopping? Having coffee at a sidewalk cafe? Enjoying a museum exhibit? Riding bikes? Rock climbing? Create as many details as you can about the location, what you are wearing, what the weather is like. Imagine yourself laughing, sharing jokes, looking into each other's eyes, telling stories. If you want, you can imagine specific people, but don't feel pressured to do that; how you feel in this scene is what matters. Ultimately, your "vibe" will attract people. What becomes so real in your mind, will become real in your physical reality. Do you doubt this? What is your current situation? What did you continually imagine, until it became real? (Again: what you learned, or did, can be unlearned, and undone).

6. **Engage your senses.** What do you see around you? Hear? Taste? Smell? Touch? This will help you make the scene even more real.

7. **"Feel it real."** What emotions would you feel if you were surrounded by friends right now? Allow those feelings to build and build within you, as you put yourself in the picture. Let yourself feel how relaxed you *are*, how happy you *are*, how comfortable you *are* talking with your friend(s). If you feel relief at having so many great friends *now*, let yourself feel relief. If you feel love, let that feeling build while you imagine love radiating out from your heart toward other people. Feel gratitude for having such wonderful friends. Let your heart swell with love and gratitude as you visualize sharing your life with other people. The more realistic you can make your visualization and the more feeling you put into it, the better.

8. **Reinforce it with words.** You can whisper "thank you" or "I love you" as you do your visualization. Imagine yourself

silently thanking your friends for their presence in your life. Imagine them saying "thank you" and "I love you" to you as well.

9. **Explore these images and feelings as long as you can.** In the beginning it will be hard to stay focused but that's okay; you can reinforce the visualization throughout the day and eventually it *will* become part of the way you think. The more you practice visualizing what you want, the more real it will become in your mind; and then, your behaviors will naturally follow.

10. **Do not repeat the same visualization each time.** In the beginning, stick to one social situation that you want to experience perfectly. But as you do this over the coming weeks, add different situations. Visualizing a variety of social situations will be more effective than sticking to one situation. You want to make it clear to your mind that you *are* surrounded by friends at work, school, the gym, your neighborhood, a group you belong to, your house of worship… anywhere you normally frequent.

What you are doing in this exercise is mentally rehearsing yourself already as part of a wonderful group of friends, in the present tense.

The more you practice this, the more you create a strong emotional affinity with the *idea* of being surrounded by friends. These strong emotions (joy, contentment, relief, love, etc.) will make you feel like a person who makes friends very easily; and then, your behaviors will naturally follow!

As often as you can, mentally rehearse yourself already enjoying the company of others. This is a great exercise to do in times when you are doing something that does not require a lot of attention, such as walking, showering, or folding laundry.

The most important part of the visualization is the *feelings*.

The Self-Talk Exercise

"Worry is a thin stream of fear trickling through the mind. If encouraged, it cuts a channel into which all other thoughts are drained." ~ Arthur Somers Roche

Many people will insist that they never talk to themselves, and that saying positive affirmations is a waste of time.

If this sounds like you; if you believe that you never talk to yourself; if you believe that your self-talk does not influence your decisions, ask yourself this:

What do you do when you worry?

Is the bad scenario that you worry about just images and feelings, or *do you discuss the problem in your mind and what could happen?*

Words lead to feelings. Feelings lead to actions. Actions lead to results.

For example, let's say you had an experience where someone rejected you when you asked them out. You replay the scene over and over in your head, right? Each time you do this, the feelings of hurt and resentment build. Pretty soon, the narrative in your mind starts to center around whether you are good enough, whether you will end up alone, whether you are too ugly, too stupid, too whatever... and the more you reinforce these thoughts, the more powerful they become. Eventually you will convince yourself that you are simply not good enough to even ask anyone out.

In the example above, you have consciously or unconsciously *agreed* that it is extremely difficult *for you* to get a date. Whenever you affirm, "It's hard to get a date," you are stating what you believe to be a fact... a fact based on experience and your inner narrative about the situation.

Every time you add a verbal description to an image or a feeling, you reinforce that *"this is how things are."*

Affirmations can be positive or negative. They are simply interpretations of a situation that you repeat often enough to make them feel real.

The point is that you are already saying affirmations all the time! Even if you say, "I don't believe that affirmations work," that's an affirmation!

The important thing is to ensure that your self-talk—your affirmations—support you or hold you back.

Whether your automatic affirmations are positive or negative, they often become self-fulfilling prophecies.

Let's talk about likability. You might have been rejected by someone in the past and told yourself it is because you are not good-looking; and when you compare yourself to people who are good-looking and are surrounded by people, you start to believe that it must be true. Even if it is just that this popular person is a celebrity!

Remember: if you repeat *any* statement often enough, you will start to believe it!

If you tell yourself, "I'm not lovable" often enough because a potential date said no, you communicate to yourself that you shouldn't even bother dating.

You are already very, very good at affirmations.

"It's not what we say out loud that really determines our lives. It's what we whisper to ourselves that has the most power." ~ Robert Kiyosaki

In fact, all of us are *world-championship-level experts* at talking ourselves into and out of situations.

So it makes sense that if you are talking yourself out of going to a party or striking up a conversation, you have to retrain yourself to talk yourself *into* taking the actions that will make new friends.

In this exercise, you will be replacing self-defeating self-talk with empowering self-talk. Repeat the affirmations during your morning and evening visualization exercises and reinforce these statements throughout the day (whenever you remember).

It's important to follow these instructions to the letter because simply saying "I am" statements (for example, "I am friendly" or "I make friends easily") can feel like a giant lie given the current circumstances. This will spark a lot of resistance. It won't feel right, and so you will quit before the idea has a chance to sink in.

We are using an extremely powerful affirmations technique that really works because it introduces an idea from multiple points of view.

While there are only a few ideas in total, you will notice that for each idea, there are four affirmations plus three questions, all in the present tense but worded differently to help minimize cognitive dissonance (ideas that go against your beliefs, and are therefore rejected):
1. *"I am"* (to get used to saying empowering things about yourself)

2. *"You are"* (second person, because we tend to believe what others say about us)
3. *"(Your name) is"* (third person, also because we believe what others say about us)
4. *"It is"* or *"it feels"* (to convey "this is the way things are")

Questions prompt your brain to find proof, making it easier to adopt an idea:

5. *"Why am I...?"*
6. *"Why are you...?"*
7. *"Why is (your name)...?"*

You will get the best results if you use all of the variations each time you say the affirmations. Together, this combination of affirmations/questions will reprogram your brain to become an amazingly likable person (with you in charge, or course).

Challenge

Read through this entire challenge before starting, so you know what to expect. To prevent overwhelm, do just one set of affirmations at a time. It's much easier to get used to micro-habits that take just a few minutes than to suddenly introduce huge time-consuming habits that you will drop the minute they become inconvenient.

Choose *one set* of affirmations to work with for the next 30 days (there's no particular order to these, just choose one you like).

Write each series down on a card or piece of paper (or put them in the note section of your phone) so you can take them with you wherever you go.

For extra impact, you could also write them in your own handwriting (this engages a different part of the brain than typing on a keyboard and helps them absorb into your subconscious mind).

You can also post them somewhere you will see them often in passing.

You can say the affirmations while doing your visualization exercise but not in the beginning. It's really a lot for your mind to focus on both, so do one exercise at a time (whichever you prefer).

How to say affirmations:

1. **Say the entire group of affirmations for one idea *with feeling and with a smile on your face* several times while you are in a relaxed and happy state.** It does not matter if you believe that they are true now... remember the visualization exercise? You can say affirmations while imagining yourself in the ideal state: surrounded by people who love and appreciate you. With enough repetition, you will start to feel that what you say is real!

2. **Repeat the set as many times each day as you can, for a minimum of 30 days** to allow your brain to create new neural pathways and reinforce them, so that these thoughts become just as automatic as the negative thoughts you are thinking now. With enough repetition, these new ideas will begin to override your old conditioning. Truly, you will become a new you!

Idea 1: I am a likable person.
- I am a likable person.
- You are a likable person.
- (Your name) is a likable person.
- It is possible to be a likable person.
- Why am I so likable?
- Why are you such a likable person?
- Why is (your name) such a likable person?

Idea 2: It's easy to make friends.
- I make friends easily.
- You make friends easily.
- (Your name) makes friends easily.
- It is fun to make friends so easily.
- Why is it so easy for me to make friends?
- Why is it so easy for you to make friends?
- Why is it so easy for (your name) to make friends?

Idea 3: I feel confident meeting new people.
- I feel confident meeting new people.
- You feel confident meeting new people.
- (Your name) feels confident meeting new people.
- It is possible to feel confident meeting new people.
- Why am I so confident meeting new people?
- Why are you so confident meeting new people?
- Why is (your name) so confident meeting new people?

Idea 4: People like me.
- People like me.
- People like you.
- People like (your name).
- It is nice to know that people like me.
- Why do people like me?
- Why do people like you?
- Why do people like (your name)?

Idea 5: I am grateful to have such good friends.
- I am grateful to have such good friends.
- You are grateful to have such good friends.
- (Your name) is grateful to have such good friends.
- It feels heartwarming to have such good friends.
- Why do I have such good friends?
- Why do you have such good friends?
- Why does (your name) have such good friends?

Idea 6: It's fun to be around other people.
- I like to be around other people.
- You like to be around other people.
- (Your name) likes to be around other people.
- It's fun to be around other people.
- Why is it so fun for me to be around other people?
- Why is it so fun for you to be around other people?
- Why is it so fun for (your name) to be around other people?

Idea 7: I am relaxed in social situations.
- I feel relaxed in social situations.
- You feel relaxed in social situations.
- (Your name) feels relaxed in social situations.
- Social situations are relaxing and fun.
- Why do I feel so relaxed in social situations?
- Why do you feel so relaxed in social situations?
- Why does (your name) feel so relaxed in social situations?

The secret to using affirmations successfully is to say them with deep emotion (joy and gratitude) in the present tense, as if it were already true.

Again, if you can imagine yourself alone and lonely, you can imagine yourself perfectly content and happy, surrounded by a great group of friends. It just takes practice and consistent repetition before you believe it.

Get clear on how you want to feel as a socially confident person with a lot of good friends. Then, recreate that feeling each time you mentally rehearse making friends, and each time you say your affirmations.

The Final Secret: Gratitude and Relief

"I awoke this morning with devout thanksgiving for my friends, the old and the new." ~ Ralph Waldo Emerson

Two of the most important emotions that will drive your behaviors from now on, are gratitude and relief. These are both emotions that are deeply felt when you are surrounded by people who love and appreciate you.

<u>Challenge</u>

Every morning and evening as part of your mental rehearsal and affirmations, express gratitude. You do not have to make an exhaustive list but do get in the habit of naming at least five things you are grateful for each day... and *why* you are grateful for them. Just making a list of things isn't as powerful as acknowledging why you are grateful for something.

This has an exceptional way of tuning you in to seeing the silver linings in loneliness, rejection, social awkwardness, shyness, and so on. These things aren't in your life to drag you down. They are here to teach you and ultimately elevate you.

Like affirmations and visualization, always make feelings of gratitude and relief in the present tense.

Let yourself feel gratitude. Let yourself feel relief knowing that your life is so much sweeter and richer (not to mention a lot less lonely) when you have good friends.

When you are doing your mental rehearsal, focus on bringing these two feelings up as much as possible. But don't stop there. Every chance you get, express gratitude, and learn to find feelings of relief when even the smallest things in life go well.

Appreciate the people in your life. Be grateful for experiences and mistakes that have opened your heart. Appreciate everything you take for granted. As you go through this book, get used to adding friendship to your list of everyday things you are grateful for. Thinking about your new connections as though you already have them, lumped in with your cozy home and everything else that is already yours, will accelerate integrating the idea of already having friends into your other-than-conscious mind.

Repetition: Where the Magic Happens

"It's the repetition of affirmations that leads to belief. And once that belief becomes a deep conviction, things begin to happen." ~ Muhammad Ali

Progress is encouraging, so keep a progress journal during your 30-day challenge. Once you've reached the 30-day mark, take note of any differences in how you feel, speak, or approach others.

Challenge

After 30 days you will have gone through one set of affirmations as well as a month of visualizations. Choose another set of affirmations and repeat this entire exercise for another month along with your daily mental rehearsal.

You will notice there are seven sets of affirmations so that means seven months of daily exercises.

However, don't pressure yourself to do all seven months! Adding more stress to your life is counterproductive.

Simply commit to just one 30-day period. If you like the results, add another month. Each time you add 30 days, it will be easier and more natural.

Don't worry about "when" you will experience the shift and start to feel like someone who can easily make friends. That all depends on the emotional effort you put in with these exercises; how consistent you are with your daily practice; and patience, while simultaneously working on the other methods outlined in this book. "When" is impossible to say, but every day you will be closer to becoming a confident and supremely likable person who easily makes friends everywhere.

As much as you can, keep going beyond the 30-day challenge. Why? Because no thought pattern or belief exists on its own. Each belief is linked to other beliefs in a complex web, and something can always disrupt situations where you now feel comfortable. Little by little as you create empowering beliefs, you will notice that the "attached" beliefs will also start to change.

Chapter 4: One Connection at a Time

Social Connection if You Aren't an Extrovert

"All life is an experiment. The more experiments you make the better." ~ Ralph Waldo Emerson

Developing the traits of a likable person isn't difficult. You may need to practice developing the mindset and hone some of the traits more than others, but you can do it (we'll outline the steps later in the book).

The trick is, where will you actually go to meet people? And how do you make connections if you are shy or introverted?

Everyone needs human connection, whether you identify as an extrovert or introvert, or outgoing or shy. But "how" you make connections will be a little different for everyone.

If you are an introvert, or shy (they are not the same), you probably cringe at those cutesy lists of how to become more social and where to meet people. Advice such as:
- Join a club or MeetUp group
- Introduce yourself to your neighbors
- Join a gym
- Join a dance class
- Join a book club
- Take your dog to a dog park
- Go to bars with games like Trivia night
- Join a religious or spiritual group
- Pick a person at a party and introduce yourself
- Join the local Chamber of Commerce

- Join a networking group
- Go to a music, art, or food festival

These are things that outgoing extroverts would do naturally, but they go completely against the grain of how shy people operate. *Are you supposed to just walk up and introduce yourself?*

Lists like this are terrifying to anyone who suffers from shyness, or who just does not like initiating social interaction. We'll get into some tips on how to overcome shyness shortly. You can make great friends even if you are very shy!

What about introversion? Isn't that the same thing as being shy? It's not the same at all.

- Introverts want to be with others, but only to a point (they recharge in solitude). Introverts may be outgoing and friendly, painfully shy, or anywhere in between. Introverts are generally reserved and won't warm up until they have a reason to. Introverts dislike crowds, hate small talk, and are easily overstimulated with too much social interaction. Introverts prefer to have fewer, but deeper, connections than extroverts, so they may have a small handful of close friends (which their extroverted friends find baffling).

- Shy people want to be with others, but fear that they will be rejected and don't know how to connect. Shy people may be introverted, extroverted, or anywhere in between. Initiating contact is excruciating for a shy person. They are generally fine once a conversation starts, especially if it is one-on-one and the other person is warm and friendly.

What's important is that everyone needs social connections. How individuals go about making those connections will be quite different from person to person.

But let's throw out the labels, because they can just cause more anxiety.

The Best Approach, Whoever You Are: Make One Connection at a Time

"Think back to the most important experiences of your life, the highest highs, the greatest victories, the most daunting obstacles overcome. How many happened to you alone? I bet there are very few. When you understand that being connected to others is one of life's greatest joys, you realize that life's best comes when you initiate and invest in solid relationships." ~ John C. Maxwell

The best approach for forging new connections is simple and it works for anyone, whether you are an extrovert, introvert, outgoing, or shy: one connection at a time.

Meeting one person is about as non-threatening as any social interaction gets, even for shy people.

In later chapters we'll talk about specific steps to take on how to mold yourself into a truly likable person. For now, though, let's talk about where to find people to connect with outside of parties and other social gatherings. These solutions offer an alternative to situations where you actually have to walk up and introduce yourself.

Online

"A friend may be waiting behind a stranger's face." ~ Maya Angelou

If you are worried about meeting new friends in person, there's nothing wrong with starting a conversation online. In fact, in the modern age this can be a lifesaver for anyone who's shy or feels socially awkward.

A friend told me a story about how she met her best friend on Facebook.

My friend is a semi-professional photographer, and one day another photographer's ad popped up in her feed. She liked what she saw and liked the page. A few weeks later after browsing this photographer's portfolio and liking a few posts, my friend noticed that this photographer was also a passionate cyclist.

She decided to reach out via messenger. Even though they lived over a thousand miles away, my friend—whom I would classify as an introvert and a little on the shy side—reached out to this new connection and sparked a conversation.

For my friend, it was completely non-threatening because it was a connection made online. Even if there was a chance of rejection, it wasn't a face-to-face rejection and so, very little risk.

In fact, realistically, due to the geographical distance, there was only a slim chance they would ever actually meet in person. And yet, their friendship grew and eventually they did meet. They have been very close friends for over ten years now.

The conversation-starter my friend used was simple: shared interests. A few genuine compliments, and some open-ended questions.

What's nice about online friendships is that you can get to know a little about people, and chances are you have mutual acquaintances or friends, so you automatically have something to spark a conversation—very unlike the awkwardness of meeting someone at a party, where you know nothing about the person.

Once the ice is broken (and on social media, that's not that hard to do), then using the techniques you will learn about in this book, you can start conversations that could lead to wonderful personal connections.

Challenge

If you are on social media, there are always suggestions for new connections. Take some time to browse through these suggestions and reach out. Take the chance. You already have some common ground to talk about—something that caught your eye about this person—and really, since it is not face-to-face, even if it does not go anywhere, it is far easier than a face-to-face meeting that fizzles.

If they accept your friend request, send a simple message with a friendly hello and a note about one of their posts. See where it goes.

Volunteering

"The best way to find yourself is to lose yourself in the service of others." ~ Gandhi

What's brilliant about meeting people while you are volunteering is that the focus is not on you. The focus is on a mutually important cause. You just show up, get to work, there's no pressure to start a conversation about something unrelated, and once you've spent a little time with a group of people, you might naturally gravitate toward one or several. It's an easy, organic way of connecting through a shared interest.

Challenge

If you haven't volunteered before, start. Even if you don't go there with the purpose of meeting people, you will feel good because you are helping.

If you currently volunteer, always arrive with a smile on your face. Volunteering can be mentally or physically hard, so always keep your focus on how you are helping. The more positive your attitude, the more you will enjoy the experience and the more you will be seen as likable. A good attitude is contagious!

Making Friends in Social Situations That You Would Go to Anyway

"Every time you are tempted to react in the same old way, ask if you want to be a prisoner of the past or a pioneer of the future." ~ Deepak Chopra

Most of us have a set pattern in how we approach social situations. For example, you may seek out the host. Or, you may say quick hellos and then gravitate toward the buffet table and stay there until someone talks to you. Or, you shadow the person you came with and let them guide the social interactions. What's your style?

If you are in a social situation you would be in anyway, such as an office party or a close friend's wedding, here's how you can make the best of the situation and meet a new friend or two (or more).

<u>Challenge</u>

Do something different than you would normally do. Here are some ideas:
- Arrive early so you can strike up a conversation with the one person who also shows up early. By the time more people arrive, you will be in full swing with a conversation that others may join.
- Get a drink before approaching anyone (light alcohol use has been called a "social lubricant").
- Wear a conversation-starter outfit. If being outlandish isn't your style, that's okay! One wardrobe piece such as a bold

necklace or a T-shirt from an exotic place is often enough to break the ice.
- Stand by yourself. It's easy, if you are shy! Chances are you are not the only one who's having trouble approaching people. It's easier to approach a small group than a large one, and even easier to approach an individual than a small group. If you are by yourself at the buffet or admiring your host's artwork—and you have a pleasant look on your face and open body language—you increase the chance of someone approaching you.
- Make room to invite other people to join. If you are standing in a circle engaged in conversation, you can physically make room for others to join. Open your posture in a welcoming way by putting a little space between yourself and the person next to you, and by angling your body slightly out of the circle.

Anywhere You Normally Frequent

"You can't stay in your corner of the Forest waiting for others to come to you. You have to go to them sometimes." ~ A. A. Milne, *Winnie-the-Pooh*

The "mere-exposure effect" suggests that people are more apt to like other people who are familiar, even just casually. This means you can meet people anywhere you normally go, just by making yourself familiar.

In a University of Pittsburgh study, four women of similar appearance were asked to pose as students in a psychology class and asked not to interact with other students. One woman did not attend class at all, one woman attended 5 classes, one attended 10 classes, and one attended 15 classes. When researchers later showed male students pictures of the four women, the men indicated greater affinity toward the women they had seen more often in class.

Exposure had greater effects on similarity and attraction, which indicates that simply being in a place you normally go, increases your chances of striking up a conversation with others who also frequent that place.

For example, simply going to the gym, coffee shop, or bookstore regularly makes you more likely to be approached than someone who attends less often.

<u>Challenge</u>

This week choose one location that you regularly frequent, and practice initiating nonverbal connections with people. Simply smile, make eye contact, and say "hi." Don't pressure yourself to take it any further. Just make it a point to create subtle connections. The other person may initiate a conversation, or perhaps you will; but if not, that's okay. The more times you see someone and "invite them in" with a friendly smile and a hello, the more likely they are to develop a greater affinity toward you.

Chapter 5: First Impressions: Welcome and Ease

Breaking Down Barriers

"Whether with a new acquaintance or an existing relationship, stay open to the possibility that your perceptions aren't entirely accurate; it just may give you the opportunity to strengthen the bond." ~ Michelle Tillis Lederman

Have you ever met someone and instantly felt a connection; or, met someone and instantly felt repelled? Sometimes you know why, but sometimes the answers aren't as obvious: just a gut feeling.

As the old saying goes, first impressions last. A bad first impression can be nearly impossible to undo, and it sets the tone for any interaction or relationship that follows. You will learn an amazing skill in this chapter: how to overcome your first bad impression with someone. This will make you likable in their eyes.

What's ironic is that first impressions are made within seconds, and they are powerful.
When meeting someone for the first time, the brain works extremely quickly to form an opinion about someone based on appearance, body language, mannerisms, and demeanor. A study examined volunteers who were shown hundreds of pictures of various objects and animals. When asked to identify animal images, the volunteers' brains registered recognition of animals within one-tenth of a second.

The visual cortex, which processes visual information, works incredibly fast; much faster than the more complex parts of the brain that analyze the data. The immediate response of the visual cortex is to classify something (or someone). The visual cortex gets an instant "read" on a person, encoding social information well before the more logical parts of the brain (which evaluate the data) have even had their morning coffee.

According to Dr. James Bednar of the University of Edinburgh's School of Informatics, "These results have far-reaching implications for explaining our sensory experience. They show that whenever we open our eyes, enter a room, or go around a corner we can quickly get the gist of a scene, well before figuring out exactly what we are looking at."

The fast process of forming a first impression is a complex cognitive feat. Each new person comes with a set of complex and often ambiguous information, so our first "snap" judgment is simply: "I like you" or "I don't like you."

Are first impressions accurate? Generally, yes. From an evolutionary perspective, a first impression had to be made quickly to determine whether a stranger was a threat, an ally, or a potential mate. Even today, the first thing we become aware of is whether we like someone or not.

The first skill to learn when it comes to making friends is how to make a positive first impression.

If you make a good first impression, you immediately make someone feel at ease. This opens the door to a positive interaction and friendship. Here's how to hone your first-impression skills:

Relax!

"Right now, someone you haven't met is out there wondering what it would be like to meet someone like you." ~ Unknown

Almost everyone gets a little nervous when meeting someone new, and this can lead to nervous habits like nail-biting, the inability to hold someone's gaze, or sweaty palms.

Think about the quote in this section, and approach the situation from that perspective: What if fate brought you together? What if it is not a coincidence that the two of you should meet in this very instant?

Your attitude helps, but there are physical ways to "cue" a positive and relaxed attitude. You can use a relaxation technique before any social interaction to make it less stressful, and to prime your mind for making what could be a once-in-a-lifetime connection.

Calm Mind, Peaceful Mind

"Being relaxed, at peace with yourself, confident, emotionally neutral, loose, and free-floating—these are the keys to successful performance in almost everything."
~ Wayne Dyer

Use this powerful self-soothing technique before a social situation: close your eyes and turn them gently inward (crossing them very slightly) and upward. Imagine you are looking out through your third eye, which is a point just above and between the eyebrows.

Breathe deeply as you do this, focusing on a long, slow, and complete exhale. Imagine all your anxiety leaving you with each exhale. Push it all out. Let the inhale take care of itself. Do this until you feel calm and positive.

You may notice that your mental chatter slows or even stops; and if you are not thinking, you can't be worrying about what will happen or what people will think.

When you are in a social situation and think that people are judging you... know that they have already judged you, just as you have judged them, in those first few seconds of meeting. After that, they are only concerned about how you perceive them, just as you are worried about how they will perceive you.

The Power Pose

"Confidence is deciding you are unstoppable—not that you will never fail." ~ Tom Bilyeu

Leonardo DaVinci's famous drawing, "The Vitruvian Man," is a great example of a Power Pose. This stance—with legs wider than hip-width and outstretched to the sky (basically making an X)—has been proven to increase testosterone production if you hold it for at least 2 minutes. Testosterone is the male hormone (both males and females produce testosterone in varying amounts) and one of the results of a testosterone boost is that it increases confidence!

Hold the Power Pose for more than 2 minutes before any social situation like a party, interview, or even a date; and you will walk into the situation feeling more confident.

Showing up confidently in a social situation takes practice. Wherever possible, go to parties or events with a friend so that you always feel like you have someone to talk to.

Challenge

If you are going solo, try these confidence boosters:
- Do the Power Pose before you go.
- Visualize easily meeting people and having enjoyable conversations.
- Enter the room with a warm smile.

- Imagine you are there to learn about other people: it is your curiosity about people that draws you to them (rather than imagining yourself in the spotlight).
- Ask the good questions. Nearly everyone else is just as nervous as you. Really, most people are, if it is a situation where they don't know a lot of people. You will notice the people that have the most success in conversation are the ones asking the best questions. Be one of them.

Be on Time

"It is difficult to prove yourself reliable when people are required to wait for you."
~ Wes Fesler

If the meeting involves a scheduled time, never be late. Nobody cares about your "good excuses" no matter how legitimate they are. By being late, you are showing disrespect for the person's time, and therefore they are less inclined to like you. Arriving too early is much better than arriving late.

Challenge

If you habitually run late, challenge yourself to arrive ten minutes early. While you are waiting, you can do a relaxation exercise to ease any anxiety you may feel. The bonus of arriving early is that people tend to trickle in one by one, and everyone is looking to connect. It's much easier to arrive early and make a connection one-on-one than to enter a bustling room where people are already in groups or pairs.

Look Good

"Dress yourself to define yourself." ~ Debasish Mridha
"Looking good" is not about beauty; it is about making it clear to others that you like yourself through good hygiene and grooming, and wearing clothes that you feel good in.

Looking good is simply about dressing for the part you want to play, not the part you are playing now.

Put some effort into your appearance. You do not have to wear the latest fashions, expensive clothes, status symbols like watches, or even makeup.

Remember the power of first impressions! The first impression, if you don't care about your appearance, is off-putting. It says, loud and clear, "If you don't care about yourself, how can you possibly care about others?"

And on the flip side, overdressing or dressing too formally will make you seem uptight and stuffy.

Remember that the brain passes rapid judgment of people based on appearance. A disheveled, smelly appearance is a physical turn-off because our primitive brains categorize a filthy appearance as mental illness, parasites, disease, and poverty. These in turn imply (fairly or not) that this person is a social burden rather than a benefit to society, and they automatically repel others.

By contrast, looking good implies high status as well as social awareness, self-awareness, and self-discipline: some highly attractive traits.

They say that a picture is worth a thousand words. The picture someone sees when they look at you (your appearance), speaks volumes! Show up dressed appropriately for the occasion; be well-groomed.

Challenge

For one week, dress "one step" nicer than you normally do. Don't go from jeans and a T-shirt to business attire; but put on a nicer shirt, not your comfiest beat-up shoes, etc. Take note throughout the day how you feel about yourself. Also gauge people's reactions to you.

Communicate "I'm Friendly" with a Smile

"Because of your smile, you make life more beautiful." ~ Thich Nhat Hanh

Use positive and friendly body language when you meet someone (we'll get into details more in the next chapter). Face the person directly, make eye contact, stand tall, and greet the person with a firm handshake (or air-kiss on the cheeks, whichever is appropriate) and a genuine smile.

Most of all… your warm, friendly smile will open the door to connection.

A smile is one of the first indicators of confidence, and confidence is attractive.

In a University of Wyoming study of nearly 100 undergraduate women, participants were asked to look at photos of a woman in one of four poses: smiling with an open body position; not smiling with an open body position; smiling with a closed body position; and not smiling with a closed body position. Almost universally, the photos of the woman smiling were liked most, whether her body position was open or closed.

The *first thing* we notice about someone new is whether they are approachable. And nothing signals this better than a friendly smile.

Don't underestimate the power of a smile! A warm, genuine, confident smile helps put the other person at ease.

The term for how powerfully people influence each other's moods is called emotional contagion. You've noticed how someone can walk into a room of happy people and immediately bring everyone down; and vice versa. We can all unconsciously feel the emotions of people around us. We unconsciously mimic others' movements and facial expressions, which influences our feelings.

Challenge

Try this now: Go stand in front of the mirror and put on an angry face. Look as angry as you can. Within seconds, you will start to *feel* angry, and you will start thinking of things that fuel your anger even though just seconds ago you were perfectly happy. Next, put on a sad face. Again, within seconds you will start to *feel* sad, even though there is nothing wrong. This is how powerfully we influence each other! Now, put a big smile on your face and hold it. See how quickly you can turn your blues into bright sunshine with just a smile!

Overcoming RBF

"There is a characteristic INTJ expression which has become popularly termed 'the death glare.' This facial expression is actually not a glare, but the INTJ's neutral face." ~ Anna Moss

You may be familiar with a term, "Resting Bitch Face" or RBF, which is unfortunately most commonly applied to women. People whose faces are naturally angled downward (downcast eyes, downturned corners of the mouth, a furrowed brow, etc.) look perpetually upset and therefore less approachable.

You know you have RBF if you are often asked questions like this even when you are perfectly happy:
- Are you angry?
- Are you upset?
- Rough night, eh?
- Is something wrong?
- Want to talk about it?
- Did I say something to offend you?
- Why don't you smile more?

RBF can impact your ability to make friends because so much of your approachability lies in your facial expressions.

If you are often concentrating hard at work and your face conveys intense concentration, you are less likely to appear friendly and approachable than those who always seem to be smiling.

Unfortunately, your expression is *not* a clear indication of your emotions. Behavioral scientist Jason Rogers found that the average neutral face only expresses about 3% of hidden emotions. People with RBF, however, show one emotion in particular that leads to the "bitch" classification: *contempt*.

For whatever reason, whether it is actual concentration, fatigue, facial structure, or just muscle habits (such as after years of chronic stress), you could feel perfectly happy and look irritated, tired, or upset.

People who are considered to have RBF tend to look contemptuous or judgmental even when their emotions are neutral. And who wants to be with someone who holds them in contempt, someone who's judging them negatively? Even without showing judgment or contempt, who wants to be around someone who looks irritated? Who wants to extend an invitation to someone who perpetually looks like they are about to burst into tears?

It could simply be that your facial structure is such that your mouth naturally raises on one side when you are resting, causing a contemptuous expression, or naturally turns downward, causing an upset expression.

In Western society, it is unfortunate to be a woman with RBF. Women are expected to get along with others, and there is more pressure to constantly smile. In fact, it makes people far more uncomfortable when a woman isn't smiling than when a man is not smiling. Forcing a smile feels fake (and can even make people look more contemptuous), so it can seem like there's no way out.

But not all is lost. Here's how you can overcome RBF.

Challenge

1. When you are looking at someone, try to look up at them. Obviously, this is easier if they are taller than you or if they are standing while you sit. Upturned eyes look more curious (i.e., interested in the speaker) and therefore more receptive. If you are the taller one, you could try turning your face downward slightly and looking up; or make an excuse to sit. Even if you are both seated, height differences tend to be less noticeable than when people are standing.

2. Adopt a Mona Lisa smile, training the muscles around your mouth to lift themselves into a small smile. Do this as often as you can during the day. In conversation, consciously try to hold a smile more often.

3. Get in the habit of smiling more. Every time you look at yourself in the mirror, smile… and most importantly, hold that smile until you can't help but laugh. This is a powerful mood and confidence booster! Even a smile that starts off fake will signal the brain that "the other person" (you, in the mirror) is smiling, and therefore all is well. Feel-good chemicals will be released, and pretty soon you will be smiling a genuine "Duchenne" smile where the corners of your eyes crinkle (and good luck *not* giggling when you see that!).

4. Let your fake social smile blossom into a genuine smile. Many people put on a fake "social smile" when they are in a social situation where they feel uncomfortable. Both fake social smiles and overly cheesy smiles make you look insincere; once again, you can put a smile on your face before you enter the room and hold it for a minute or two—it will soon turn into a genuine smile! If you are already in the room, put a smile on your face, hold it, and think about something amusing, or simply extend warm feelings toward the person you are with. Soon, you will be smiling for real.

5. Smile when you wake up in the morning. Smile when something good happens (even the little things). Smile when you talk on the phone (even over the phone, people can tell if you are smiling or not). Smile when you exercise. Smile when you take care of yourself. Smile in the shower. The more you smile, the more you start to see that life is good, and that's an extremely attractive vibe!

Put People at Ease

"We don't meet people by accident. They are meant to cross our paths for a reason." ~ Unknown

Putting people at ease makes you more likable. Here are three tips for making people feel relaxed and comfortable around you:

Make Yourself Scarce

"There's only one thing more precious than our time and that's who we spend it on." ~ Leo Christopher

When you meet someone who appears hesitant to make your acquaintance, make it clear that you only have a minute because you have another engagement in a few minutes. This counterintuitive move immediately puts people at ease because they know that if the conversation is not going well, they know they have an "out" (as do you). And if the conversation does go well and there's a connection, you could always look at your phone and say that your engagement just got canceled.

It can also convey that you are likable and/or important.

Start with an icebreaker

"What is your favorite dinosaur?" ~ You, using an icebreaker

Starting a conversation with a stranger is not always easy if there isn't an obvious topic. Prepare a few questions ahead of time that you could use in any social situation where there are not obvious topics in common. In Chapter 7, we'll share some great icebreakers to lighten the mood and get people talking.

For now, the world's best icebreaker to lighten the mood and get people talking is "What is your favorite dinosaur?" (Yes, this is absolutely a great question to ask any adult.)

If you can't think of a verbal icebreaker, wear one. A bold piece of jewelry, a work-of-art tie, a witty T-shirt, a cool hat, or even a pair of fun shoes are topics that people can comfortably comment on.

Depending on the situation, you could also bring a conversation piece such as your dog, a dish you cooked, or a specialty cocktail you created.

Take Interest

"When two people talk with mutual respect and listen with a real interest in understanding another point of view, when they try to put themselves in the place of another, to get inside their skin, they change the world, even if it is only by a minute amount, because they are establishing equality between two human beings." ~ Theodore Zeldin

Many people act reserved when they first meet someone. they are not sure if they will like you (and vice versa). You can break down this barrier by encouraging them to talk about themselves. Most people will give you an "in" by revealing something about themselves: their career, their kids, etc. Ask a few friendly questions like, "I would love to hear more about that. I've always been curious about (the topic they have introduced).

When you meet someone, take the attitude that someone you meet is meant to cross your path… and it is your mission to find out why. This does not mean you start interrogating them; it is more of a subtle change in attitude that is open and welcoming instead of reserved. Be the one to take the wall down by showing interest in the person.

Broaden the Small Talk

"That's all small talk is—a quick way to connect on a human level—which is why it is by no means as irrelevant as the people who are bad at it insist. In short, it is worth making the effort." ~ Lynn Coady

Small talk can only carry a conversation for a very short time. You have to get beyond it at some point, and asking the right questions helps you be more likable.

Ask for stories, not answers.

Getting beyond small talk means asking questions that invite stories, not just a "yes" or "no." Here are some examples:
- Instead of "How are you?" ask "What are you looking forward to this week?"
- Instead of "How was your day?" ask "What's the most interesting thing you did today?"
- Instead of "What do you do?" ask "How did you end up in your line of work?"
- Instead of "Would you like some wine?" ask "Where did you drink your most memorable glass of wine?"
- Instead of "Where are you from?" ask "What's the most remarkable thing about where you grew up?"
- Instead of "What's your name?" ask "What does your name mean?"
- Instead of "How long have you been living here?" ask "What's the quirkiest thing about this house?"

Challenge

The next time you are engaged in small talk with someone, ask an unusual question that encourages them to tell a story.

Use Their Name

"A person's name is to that person, the sweetest, most important sound in any language." ~ Dale Carnegie

Names are important to most of us. They represent who we are. They symbolize our identity (which is why it is important that your actions are likable and kind, so that people's memory of your name always has a positive association). And nothing sounds more heartwarming than hearing your own name said in a friendly and kind manner.

Using a person's name in conversation right after you've learned it is a good way to remember their name, and it also lets them know that you are interested enough in them to learn and remember their name.

Every time you greet someone you know, say their name instead of just "hi." And always say their name with a smile on your face.

Be Positive

"Optimism is a happiness magnet. If you stay positive, good things and good people will be drawn to you." ~ Mary Lou Retton

The first few words you say to a person can drive the direction the conversation goes. Never, ever start a conversation with a negative topic, even if you are up to your eyeballs in a stressful or serious situation (and avoid hot topics like religion, sex, and politics). Always focus on the positives rather than on the doom and gloom (we'll cover this in later chapters). Be the one who lights up the room with a positive and optimistic attitude.

Negativity is off-putting. It's good to keep this in mind during a discussion about an unpleasant situation: it is not the situation that's necessarily the problem... it is your interpretation of it and how you choose to talk about it. Putting a positive spin on bad situations usually works very well to lighten the mood (and if someone insists on dragging the conversation down again, refuse to join in).

Many people use humor to mask their nervousness or to make a difficult situation more bearable. Even if you are not a natural jokester, do what you can to lighten the mood.

If you want to make others feel happy when they are around you, do your best to communicate positive emotions (it can help to put a smile on your face before you enter a room or approach someone), and use positive words.

Challenge

Practice using the following words more often. Sprinkle them (and their variations) naturally into your speech and with regular use, you will become associated with them in the eyes of other people.

	Accept		Adorable		
	Amazing		Appreciate		
	Awesome		Beautiful		Believe
	Beloved				
	Best		Brilliant		Can (do
it)	Come (in)				
	Comfort		Community		
	Congratulation	s	Cute		
	Delightful		Delicious		Depend
	Enjoy				
	Exciting	Fabulous		Friend	
	Generous				
	Good		Gorgeous		
	Grateful		Great		
	Handsome		Happy		Help
(you)	Honor				
	Hug		Include		
	Interesting		Invite		
	Joy		Kind		Let's
		Like			

Lovable	Love	Miss	(you)
Nice			
Original	Outstanding	Peace	
Perfect			
Refreshing	Satisfying	Success	
Sweet			
Talented	Thanks	Together	
Trust			
Unique	Us	We	
Welcome			
Wonderful	Wow	Yes	
You			

What other positive words can you add to your speech? Think about things you routinely complain about and reframe them using better-feeling words. Instead of "The weather is always awful on my day off!" say something positive like, "I'm going to make the best of the weather and go to the (x) and do (y)."

Be Present

"Yesterday is history. Tomorrow is a mystery. Today is a gift. That is why it is called the present." ~ Alice Morse Earle

Within the first few seconds of meeting, you can tell if a person is present and engaged with you, or a million miles away lost in their own thoughts. And they sense the same about you.

Today, people have developed the habit of abruptly pulling out their phones and interacting with someone who's not even in the room. This is extremely thoughtless and disrespectful to the person who's right here. Set aside distractions like your phone and "be here now." Your new acquaintance deserves 100% of your attention; anything else, and they will feel unimportant.

Watch Your Proximity (Maintain Personal Space)

"Don't stand so… don't stand so… don't stand so close to me." ~ Sting

Personal space is important. Some people knowingly or unknowingly violate personal space by standing too close for comfort. Others maintain a little too much distance, which can be equally off-putting. Of course, this varies by culture and the level of intimacy you have with someone, but even within socially accepted "personal bubbles," it is important to respect someone's personal space.

Challenge

Standing too close to people is where a lot of people get into trouble, but you can follow a simple rule: stand where you are comfortable. If the person becomes visibly uncomfortable at how close you are standing to them (crossing their arms defensively, looking around in an agitated way, or stepping backwards or to the side), then you are too close!

How to Overcome a Negative First Impression

"A thousand words will not leave so deep an impression as one deed." ~ Henrik Ibsen

Negative first impressions are hard to change, but it can be done.

First: why are first impressions so "sticky"?

There is a psychological phenomenon called the "fundamental attribution error" where we quickly attribute behaviors as traits: for example, if you were rudely late for an appointment, you will be seen as someone who will always be late.

What isn't seen is what's below the surface. Maybe you didn't sleep well last night and you are having trouble concentrating. Maybe you got some bad news from your doctor and missed your exit. Maybe someone cut you off in traffic and you nearly got into an accident.

However, people aren't likely to know the reason for your performance or your attitude and sometimes they won't care. They simply assume this is how you are, and you are stuck with their negative perception of you.

Whether you are the one who holds a bad first impression or you are the one who made it, here's what you can do.

If you made a bad first impression:

Maybe you alienated a new neighbor with an off-color joke or said something to a new acquaintance that came across as condescending. It's uncomfortable, but it is not the end of the world. Here's how you can change their perception of you:

1. Give them not one, but many reasons to change their opinion of you.

Once a bad first impression has been made, it can be tempting to try to avoid the problem by avoiding the person. But this can actually make the situation worse. If you are being judged harshly and you are *not* giving them a reason to change their perception of you, then they will continue to judge you harshly.

Give them not just one, but multiple reasons to re-evaluate you. The key to this method is repetition. The essence of this is to give them so much evidence that proves that their first impression was wrong. For example, if you were late to work on your first day on a new job, you will have to be early not just once, but for many weeks.

You may need to force yourself out of your comfort zone, but it is important that you *show* them, not *tell* them, who you really are. Whatever their negative perception of you, show the opposite through repeated actions.

Challenge

Think about the last time you made an unfavorable impression on someone. If you could do something to change that first impression, what would you do to show them the real you?

Challenge yourself to have eight positive interactions with someone who is judging you unfairly. Small positive interactions are more effective than one big, dramatic event; give them *consistent* proof that their first impression was wrong. Note how long it takes them to warm up.

2. Give it time.

Sometimes, people just have to get to know you to see what you are really like. For example, a woman I know found out that one of her new coworkers was saying (behind her back) that she was "too positive." This of course hurt her deeply because this coworker saw her as fake, when in reality she was simply a cheerful person who always tried to see the best in situations and people. It was only after working together for a few months that my friend's coworker realized this is who she is, that she wasn't being fake at all.

The opposite can also be true: perhaps people label you as "standoffish" when in fact you are just shy and take a while to warm up.

If you are patient, continue to work hard, are kind and respectful, you will eventually win people over.

Of course, it is very unfair and frustrating to be classified as something you are not. However, it is helpful to remember that if you really didn't do or say anything to warrant a bad first impression, their perception of you is most often due to their own past experiences—their own baggage. Simply being your awesome self can win them over, in time.

Challenge

Think about a situation where you or someone you know was judged unfairly by someone; and over time, a friendship blossomed. Does this sound like a bad rom-com movie? It happens all the time.

If you are currently in a situation where you are being judged unfairly, give it time. If you are currently in a situation where you are judging someone unfairly, make an effort to get to know them.

3. Ask for a second chance.

It's not easy to admit wrongdoing, but it will elevate you in the eyes of others. If a bad first impression is due to something you said or did, be straightforward and say something like, "I feel like we got off to a bad start." Apologize, and ask what you can do to correct the situation.

Challenge

Think of a time you or someone you know did something wrong and did nothing to correct it. Now think of a time you or someone you know did something wrong, owned their actions, asked for forgiveness, and made an attempt to right the wrong. Which outcome was better?

4. Ask them for advice.

Showing vulnerability can make a difference. Asking for advice encourages cooperation, makes the person feel important, and shows them that you value their opinion.

Challenge

If you feel that someone doesn't like you, ask them for advice on something you know they are expert in (or at least, better or more knowledgeable than you). Take note of how their demeanor changes.

If someone made a bad impression on you:

A likable person will always give someone a second chance, whether the person asks for it or not. Here are some other tips for changing your first impression of someone; you never know when this could spark a friendship!

1. Look for the positives in them.

Nobody is all good, or all bad. Actively making an effort to see the best in people can be a game-changer in how you see others, and how you respond to them.

Challenge

Think about someone who made a bad first impression on you. Write down a list of what's positive about this person. You may have to dig a little deeper but try.

2. If they reach out, be open.

It takes courage to reach out to someone when you know they don't like you; so put yourself in their shoes! If they do reach out with an invitation, accept it.

Anna tells a story of how one of her coworkers, Roberta, spoke very badly about someone in her book club (Carrie). Based on this, Anna formed a negative first impression of Carrie. As luck would have it, Carrie invited Anna along with a mutual friend to dinner. Anna reluctantly said yes… and was very pleasantly surprised that Carrie was nothing like Roberta had said. In fact, she was an absolute delight to be with, and a friendship quickly blossomed. Anna has since pulled away from Roberta, after realizing that Roberta's toxicity was the real issue, not Carrie's personality.

Challenge

Think about a time you formed a bad impression of someone, either because of something that was said or because of your own first interaction. If the person reaches out and invites you out for drinks or an activity, give them a chance and go.

3. Give it time.

This goes both ways. Spending more time together can go either way, but you will never know unless you actually give it a chance and spend some time with this person rather than avoiding them.

<u>Challenge</u>

Think of a time you disliked someone when you first met, and how simply being around each other led to a better relationship if not a friendship.

4. Accept the apology and give them a second chance.

Showing vulnerability is difficult for many people. Some won't apologize for their mistakes; but the ones who do, should be given a chance to remedy the situation.

<u>Challenge</u>

If someone apologizes for behavior that caused you to judge them, give them a chance to make things right.

Chapter 6: Body Language

Your Body Is What People Really Pay Attention To: Not Your Words

"The body never lies." ~ Martha Graham

This chapter begins with a challenge. Body language speaks far louder than words and can make you instantly likable... or not. Begin with building awareness about the body language of people you are drawn to, and people you instinctively prefer to avoid.

The words you say should be positive, free of ego and judgment—but remember to listen closely to what your body is saying. Your nonverbal communication needs to match what you are saying.

Challenge

When we're talking about body language—which is the first thing that people notice about each other—just think about what attracts you, and what repels you. Go sit in a cafe or some public place and people-watch, especially when people are interacting with each other. Look at pictures of people in magazines or watch videos.

Start to notice the body language that makes some people approachable. Observe how they use their bodies to communicate with each other.

Then, take note of your body language when you are with others. Is it friendly and open, or closed and fearful/hostile? Even if you don't intend to come across as fearful or hostile, your body language could be telling a different story.

Of course, the most welcoming and friendly gesture you can do is smile. Here's what else you can convey nonverbally to make yourself appear approachable and friendly.

Building Rapport with Body Language

"Body language is a very powerful tool. We had body language before we had speech, and apparently, 80% of what you understand in a conversation is read through the body, not the words." ~ Deborah Bull

Ask yourself this question: How do *you* decide who to approach when you don't know anyone at a party? How do you choose whom to ask for directions? How do you choose whether to approach a booth at an art festival or keep walking by, even if you like the art?

You probably look for someone who instantly appears friendly. Your brain flash-scans and flash-processes everyone you see for potential threats and will give preference to those who seem safe and welcoming.

Without necessarily being aware why, you will automatically steer clear of people who are fidgeting, abrupt in their movements, shifty with their eyes, or nervous with their hands.

Of course, we all exhibit these behaviors when we're nervous so put yourself at ease first, so that your body language is communicating relaxed friendliness.

Open and Vulnerable = Friendly

"We tend to like each other better when walking, sitting, or standing side by side or at right angles from each other." ~ Kare Anderson

An open body language is one of the keys to becoming likable and making it easy for people to approach you. Your posture, stance, position of your arms, and facial expressions contribute to an "open" or "closed" vibe.

It's especially important to learn to be okay with being vulnerable socially by opening parts of your body that you unconsciously cover up when you are tense or angry:

- The heart: avoid standing with your arms crossed (this reads as a defensive stance). If the person you are talking to has their arms crossed, they are closed off. If you feel uncomfortable standing with your arms hanging by your sides, you can use a prop like a drink to have something to hold.

- The palms of your hands: closed fists aren't welcoming. Hands in pockets could mean a hidden weapon. Even in a friendly situation, our primal brains see closed fists or hidden hands as a threat. Keep your palms up when listening, to indicate openness to the other person's thoughts and opinions.

Closed body language could mean that you are scared, unwelcoming, or that you have something to hide. People will not approach you; and, they will find excuses to get away from you if you approach them with crossed arms or other unwelcoming body language.

Challenge

The more nervous you are, the more you need to practice openness with your body language. It helps to have a prop in your hand, such as a full glass. If there's no prop, just let your arms hang loosely at your side. There's no need to "do" anything except physically open your heart to the person standing in front of you.

Make Eye Contact

"I have a big thing with eye contact, because I think as soon as you make eye contact with somebody, you see them, and they become valued and worthy." ~ Mary Lambert

Why is eye contact so important? Eye contact means "I am present and paying attention to you." Eye contact signals interest, empathy, and can communicate that you have nothing to hide. It also signals self-control, which is extremely helpful if you are shy. If you can make yourself hold someone's gaze, you are already a step ahead of many people who suffer from shyness.

Looking everywhere except at the person you are with, is dismissive and signals that your interests lie elsewhere. It could also signal guilt, shame, or even intense shyness, none of which will draw people to you.

Learning to make comfortable eye contact takes a bit of courage and lots of practice. Practice in front of a mirror, or with people you know and feel comfortable with:
- Establish eye contact before you start speaking.
- Don't stare intently at someone (that's creepy).
- Maintain eye contact about 50% of the time while speaking and 70% of the time while listening.
- Once you have made eye contact, hold it for 4 or 5 seconds before taking a short break and then resuming eye contact.
- Be deliberate about looking away. When you look away from someone, do it easily, not as though you've just seen something fascinating behind them.

- Never look down (it signals lack of confidence and shyness).
- Never look side-to-side in jerky motions (it signals lack of trustworthiness, like you have something to hide).
- If it helps, you can look at their eyebrow instead directly at their eye, or the space between their eyes.
- Practice! Eye contact may not come easily to you, so practice in the mirror and with friends and family until you become more confident.

In certain situations, you can get out of making a lot of eye contact (such as when you are in the car with someone and you are driving) but generally you want to avoid staring at your feet, your phone, or something behind the person you are with.

Avoid wearing sunglasses in social situations, unless you really need them.

Challenge

If you are not good at holding eye contact, go to an art museum and practice looking at paintings or photographs where the subject's eyes are on you directly. You know those paintings where the eyes seem to follow you around the room. Imagine yourself holding a conversation with the subjects (especially the ones with stern faces that look like they are judging you). Follow the steps above to practice making and maintaining natural eye contact.

Eye contact makes you more likable by creating a visual connection that is impossible otherwise!

Stand Tall

"Confidence is everything, and the way you carry yourself, your posture, eye contact, all of that is such a big role in impressions, regardless of your size." ~ Camille Kostek

Standing tall makes you appear more confident, and it naturally encourages a more open and welcoming posture. Where are your shoulders? Hunched, or square? Hunched shoulders signal fear and weakness while squared shoulders signal confidence and status.

Practice standing tall; all you really need to do is lift your chest, imagining that you are opening your solar plexus which is the seat of your self-confidence... so stand tall and you will soon feel more confident.

<u>Challenge</u>

When speaking to someone, practice lifting your chest. That's all you need to do to stand taller! Yes, holding your shoulders back will help but this can cause you to be more distracted during the conversation.

What really causes you to appear slouched (from the other person's perspective) is when you allow your shoulders and chest to aim toward the floor. Simply elevate your chest and feel the openness of your solar plexus.

The Nuances of Position

"Body language is leadership at first sight." ~ Janna Cachola

The position of your body relative to the other person can convey a number of messages. You can think of your body position in three ways:

1. Face-to-face: Standing squarely facing each other, maintaining culturally appropriate distance between yourselves. Standing face-to-face is necessary to maintain eye contact. It's a confident, open, and vulnerable stance.

2. Side-by-side: If you happen to be walking alongside someone or seated next to each other on a plane or a bus, a side-by-side position still allows for eye contact, but it is a less open posture. Turning toward the other person helps establish and maintain a bond.

3. Slight angles: If facing someone directly feels too intimidating or challenging, people sometimes adopt a slightly angled position in relation to each other, for example sitting with their legs crossed and each facing each other's left shoulder. Subconsciously, this offers an "escape route" while still allowing eye contact.

You can tell a person is finished with a conversation when they change their position: they step back, turn more than a few degrees sideways, or look down or away.

Challenge

Of these stances, which one intuitively seems most likable to you: face-to-face, side-by-side, or at slight angles? If you guessed face-to-face, you are right.

Observe people you like and watch how they adjust their body position to mirror that of the person they are with. Practice this in your own conversations.

Be Still and Relaxed

"A blur of blinks, taps, jiggles, pivots, and shifts... the body language of a man wishing urgently to be elsewhere." ~ Edward R. Murrow

Of course, avoid standing as still as a robot when talking to someone, but also avoid nervous fidgeting like tapping your foot, pacing, or making repetitive or compulsive hand gestures. Anxious body language makes people tense and they will quickly make excuses to get out of the situation.

Notice that likable people are relaxed in the presence of others. How can you feel more relaxed? Focus on them! Ask questions, show genuine interest, and very soon you will forget about yourself.

<u>Challenge</u>

Notice what you do with your arms when talking to someone. Generally, having your arms hanging loosely by your side is the friendliest option (hold a drink, if that feels awkward).
- If you talk with your hands: gesticulating a little can keep a conversation animated. However, too much can make you look crazy or hyper.
- Placing your hands behind your back can make you seem regal, but distant.
- Crossing your arms signals that you are defensive, closed off, and angry.
- Lacing your fingers in front of you signals that you are attentive, interested, and comfortable.
- Placing your hands on your hips can come across as aggressive if your thumbs are facing backward (your fingers are visible at the front of your hips) or if you have made your hands into fists; if your thumbs are facing forward, it is a more relaxed stance.
- Crossing one arm across your belly with the other under your chin makes you look like you are thinking intently and if accompanied by eye contact, can signal interest in what the person is saying (this half-crossed-arms option is a good

way to wean yourself away from crossed arms if that has been a habit).

Next time you are speaking with someone, imagine that you are building a bridge between your heart and the heart of someone you've just met. Get your arms out of the way and show your friendly intentions to build that bridge.

Your Head and Face

The position of your head is important in conveying interest and friendliness. A smile and easygoing eye contact are important; but so is the angle of your face.

- A slight tilt of the head indicates interest.
- Keep your chin down slightly so that you don't look as though you are looking down your nose at someone. Keeping your chin up can also signal aggression.
- Show interest with slightly raised eyebrows, not furrowed brows which indicate stress.
- A slight Mona Lisa smile can indicate openness to someone's ideas.

Challenge

Observe likable people. How do they hold their head when they are talking to others? The next time you are in conversation with someone, practice tilting your head very slightly when they are speaking (not like a dog cocks his head; this is much more subtle).

Give the Right Physical Greeting and Use Touch Where Appropriate

"It is possible to tell things by a handshake. I like the 'looking in the eye' syndrome. It conveys interest. I like the firm, though not bone crushing shake. The bone crusher is trying too hard to 'macho it.' The clammy or diffident handshake—fairly or unfairly—gets me off to a bad start with a person." ~ George H.W. Bush

If physical touch is culturally appropriate for a particular interaction, you can use physical touch to be seen as approachable and friendly. Examples of good physical greetings include a firm handshake that doesn't crush hands; a light air-kiss on the cheeks; a touch on the shoulder; or a friendly hug.

The right touch can create an instant connection. However, unwelcome touch, especially by men to women, can be extremely off-putting.

Challenge

The next time you are speaking with someone new, you could gauge the person's receptivity to touch by smiling and saying, "I'm a hugger" and open your arms out for a hug. If they reciprocate, great! If they shrink back and say, "I'm not," then a simple handshake will do.

You can also use touch to strengthen a connection with someone you already know. If the person is receptive to touch, using subtle touch on their shoulder or arm (so light they barely notice) can make them feel comfortable.

Mirror Others

"When people are free to do as they please, they usually imitate each other." ~ Eric Hoffer

A strategy called mirroring—or subtly mimicking someone's behavior—sends an unconscious signal that "we're alike," which builds rapport. Practice subtly mirroring stances, gestures, and facial expressions. Also, be aware when you mirror someone that you like and admire. Chances are good you are unconsciously mirroring them in an effort to be like them!

A 1999 New York University study documented the "chameleon effect," which occurs when people mimic each other's behavior. Seventy-two men and women were asked to work on a task with a partner who was assigned by the researchers to either mimic or not mimic the participant's behavior (the participants were not told about whether their partner was mimicking them or not). At the end of the task, the researchers asked participants to evaluate how much they liked their partners. When the partner mimicked their behavior, participants were more likely to say that they liked their partner.

The only exception to using the mirroring strategy would be if the person is exhibiting closed or unfriendly body language. As hard as it may be to unconsciously cross your arms if theirs are crossed, resist the urge. Be the one to remain open and welcoming, and you could diffuse a tense situation and even open the door to friendship. If you mimic someone's aggressive stance or body language, you could escalate a situation; and if you mimic someone's beaten-down depressed stance, the conversation will be nothing but doom and gloom.

Humans are highly visual creatures. Mimicking behavior is actually something that most mammals do. Body language often sends a much stronger message than the spoken word and when you understand how to use body language tactics such as mirroring to build rapport, you will actually be in the driver's seat in establishing a relationship.

Challenge

Practice mirroring so that it becomes a natural part of how you interact.

***

Now that you've made a first impression and you are letting your body do a lot of the talking, it is time to learn the art of conversation that will make you instantly approachable, and will pave the way to creating new, meaningful friendships.

Chapter 7: The Art of Conversation

Be Here Now

"In general, being likeable is more about being interested—rather than interesting. Indeed, a good way to convince someone that you are an awesome conversationalist is to simply shut up and let the other person talk." ~ Karen Salmansohn

A favorable first impression can lead to great conversations, and conversations are what forge strong connections.

Icebreakers

"Just because I don't start the conversation, doesn't mean I'm not dying to speak to you." ~ Unknown

Someone has to start the conversation. Initiating conversations is often the most terrifying thing for someone who's shy, so memorizing a few great icebreakers is a great soft skill to acquire.

You will be more at ease because you will have an opening line instead of standing there awkwardly waiting for the other person to say something or scrambling to find an opening topic.

And when you initiate conversation, you will help put the other person at ease because chances are good that they don't know any great icebreakers (and they are thankful that you brought up a topic other than the weather).

Browse through this list of icebreakers, memorize a few that you like, and use them to spark conversation. Some are funny, some are serious... what's most important is that you choose ones that fit in with your personality (don't ask the dinosaur question, for example, if you don't know or care about dinosaurs).

You will notice that some icebreaker lists contain questions that end in "... and why?" Avoid using this as part of an icebreaker because it sounds more like an interview, or worse, an interrogation, than an easygoing conversation. Slip the "why" in there after the person has responded. For example, instead of "What's your favorite dinosaur and why?" open with "What's your favorite dinosaur?" and ask why later.

Tip: you can use icebreakers anytime during a conversation, to change topics or reinvigorate the conversation if it stalls.

You will notice as you read through this list of icebreakers that they are designed to encourage people to tell stories, rather than simply responding with a "yes" or a "no."

Icebreakers:
- What's your favorite dinosaur? (Yes, this is absolutely a great question to ask any adult)
- What's your favorite or most used emoji?
- In your last virtual work meeting, how many people's cats walked across the keyboard?
- Have you ever been told you look like someone famous? Who was it?
- What's the most life-changing or memorable book you ever read?
- What did you name your first car?
- If you had a time machine, would you go into the past or the future?

- If you could learn one new professional skill this year, what would it be?
- If you could write a book, what genre would it be in?
- What is your favorite thing about your job? (Or, being a parent?)
- What's your favorite mythological animal and would you want one as a pet?
- If you could bring back any fashion trend, what would it be?
- If your life was a movie, what would be your theme song?
- Who's your favorite artist (or author)?
- What's one career that you wish you could have if you were to start over today?
- If you could live anywhere for a year, where would it be?
- What is the most interesting thing you did this week?
- If you could play any movie character, who would it be?
- If you were stranded on a desert island with one person, who would it be?
- What's your favorite thing that you have found?
- If you could hop on a plane and go to your all-time favorite place, where would you go?
- Men in kilts or men in tights?
- What's your favorite building in the world?
- If you could sail around the world, what would you name your sailboat?
- What's the worst job you ever had?
- What's the weirdest thing about the place you grew up?
- What are some of the items on your bucket list?
- What's the best thing you did that you swore you would never do?
- What was the last foreign country you visited?
- What's your best scar story?
- Would you rather have the power of invisibility or flight?
- If you could choose any person from history to have dinner with, who would it be?

- If you could be any animal, what would you choose to be?
- If you could be immortal, at what age would you choose to be forever?
- If you had all the money in the world, what would be one toy that you would buy?
- What song or album could you listen to on repeat?
- What's the best thing you would put in your dream house?
- Have you ever met your doppelganger?
- What is the best dish you can cook?
- What are the three best meals you have had in your entire life?
- Do you remember any goofy commercial jingles from your childhood?

Of course, some of these icebreakers are unabashedly silly while others are more thought-provoking. Icebreakers can involve open-ended questions but even the ones that could be quickly answered often lead to deeper conversation simply because they are intriguing, especially if they are unexpected.

Choose icebreakers based on the context and the person you are speaking to. Avoid icebreakers related to sensitive topics like religion, sex, or politics. In fact, avoid these topics altogether until you know someone better.

Most of all, avoid talking about the weather (*so boring!*) unless something truly epic is happening—while weather is a go-to for many people, reverting to this topic gives the impression that you have nothing interesting to talk about. And never, ever complain about the weather. Make light of it as much as possible.

Challenge

Choose one icebreaker and practice it on new acquaintances. Since you don't know the person, you may not know which icebreaker topic to choose so just choose one that feels right to you, something you would naturally ask a friend or close acquaintance. Once you get comfortable using one icebreaker, add to your repertoire until you can comfortably spark conversation on a variety of topics.

Work, as a Conversation Topic

"The only reason why we ask other people how their weekend was is so we can tell them about our own weekend." ~ Chuck Palahniuk

What about work? Many people stick to work-related topics when they meet someone new or interact with colleagues at an office party, but this is usually due to discomfort and not knowing what else to talk about.

If you are in a professional social setting such as an office party or conference, you can use work-related topics to start a conversation but don't limit yourself to work topics unless both of you are passionate about the subject, because you will come across as boring.

People have lives outside of work and some prefer to leave their work at work and not talk about it at all outside of work.

Challenge

Use your judgment. If a work-related conversation isn't going anywhere, try one of your awesome icebreakers as a "pattern interrupt." A pattern interrupt is a change of subject that forces someone to change the thought pattern they are on. It's a proven sales technique, but it can also be useful in conversations that are stalling. Using an off-topic icebreaker question to guide the conversation in a different direction.

A Stalled Conversation Is Not Necessarily the End

"Conversation about the weather is the last refuge of the unimaginative." ~ Oscar Wilde

One of the biggest challenges to connecting with new people is the awkward silence that can pop up during a conversation. Here's how to get around it and keep the conversation going.

First, why do we run out of things to say? A number of factors can kill a conversation. Here's how to overcome conversation blocks.

You or the Other Person Simply Aren't Interested

"Nobody can make you feel inferior without your consent." ~ Eleanor Roosevelt

Sometimes, you will be rejected. That's a fact of life. But don't take it personally.

Everyone faces rejection *and everyone has dealt rejection.*

It's unreasonable to expect "everybody" to like you. Just as you will not instantly like everyone you meet, there will be those who will not like you. That's okay. Don't worry. Just move on.

<u>Challenge</u>

If it is clear your efforts aren't going anywhere, let it go. Politely excuse yourself.

The Topic Has Run Dry

"If you are ever at a loss to support a flagging conversation, introduce the subject of eating." ~ Leigh Hunt

When there's nothing more to discuss on a subject, that's okay, you have the tools to quickly change topics. Practice using the icebreaker topics (remember, use those that feel authentic to you and demonstrate a genuine interest in the other person) to restart the conversation!

<u>Challenge</u>

Food is a universally liked subject. Choose an icebreaker related to food; it is an opportunity to find out a lot about someone!

You Are Filtering (Being a Perfectionist)

"Healthy striving is self-focused: "How can I improve?" Perfectionism is other-focused: "What will they think?" ~ Brené Brown

Many people hold back from speaking until they are sure they have come up with something witty, smart, interesting, or funny. This can grind a conversation to a halt because the other person may think that silence equals lack of interest.

Nobody expects you to be a witty conversationalist. After all, you've just met. This is an opportunity to be yourself and let people get to know the real you.

<u>Challenge</u>

Be yourself and say what's on your mind as long as you are being friendly and kind.

Encourage the Other Person to Go Deeper into a Topic

"You can close more business in two months by becoming interested in other people than you can in two years by trying to get people interested in you." ~ Dale Carnegie

Not that every conversation is about business, of course… but the sentiment is the same: the more you show interest, the better the response.

Show the other person that you are really listening. Everybody loves to be heard, and they will be more likely to continue the conversation if they know you are engaged. Memorize these phrases, and use them to encourage the other person to continue:
- "That's interesting, tell me more!"
- "Wow, I didn't know that!"
- "That must have been quite the experience."

Being encouraged when someone wants to learn more feels really good.

<u>Challenge</u>

Choose a phrase that feels authentic to you, to encourage someone to go deeper into a topic. If you would never say, "That's interesting, tell me more," then rephrase it in a way that sounds good to you… and use it.

Storytelling: How to Keep a Conversation Going

"Inside each of us is a natural-born storyteller, waiting to be released." ~ Robin Moore

People are hardwired to engage when they hear stories. It's how we've shared information and experiences since the dawn of spoken language. The more interesting the story, the more memorable it is. Even better if it is awkward or funny—just use stories to spice up your conversations.

Integrate stories into the conversation, but not only stories about yourself. You don't have to draw from your own life experience. Use stories from anywhere: other people's experience, something you've seen on TV, or read in a book.

Challenge

Telling your own stories is fine, of course; just avoid making the conversation all about you. Once you've shared a story, let the other person share theirs.

Mute Yourself, to Let the Conversation Flow

"Wisdom is the reward you get for a lifetime of listening when you'd have preferred to talk." ~ Doug Larson

Very often, our inclination is to share our own stories and accomplishments when others share theirs, in an attempt to find common ground, create a bond, and be accepted.

However, this can backfire because those who always one-up people's stories come across as arrogant and self-centered. This can quickly stop a conversation because the speaker thinks, "Why bother telling you anything if it is always going to circle around to become about *you*?"

Ironically, you will hear these "I'm better than you" stories whether the original story was positive or negative. You can spot these when the listener gives only cursory attention to the speaker's story and then jumps right into their own, and it is almost always guaranteed to be "more."

Examples include: their victory was better… their divorce was uglier… their race time was faster even though their injury was worse and they were far less prepared… they flew to Europe for half the price of your ticket… they got into more trouble as a kid but their own kids are absolute angels… they overcame wayyyy bigger obstacles… they made more money than so-and-so… their plane was delayed for days not hours… their failure was more spectacular… their heartache was more crushing and they will probably never love again, etc.

This kind of dramatization and verbal competition is extremely off-putting.

Unfortunately, verbal competition is a common phenomenon that you want to watch out for. If you catch yourself responding to someone's story with one that could be taken as one-upmanship, just mute yourself.

Don't steal their thunder when they are sharing an accomplishment, and don't make it about you when they are sharing a heartbreak or admitting to a failure.

Save your stories for another time (like when you are asked) and let the person speak.

In fact, few things build rapport as much as letting people talk about their favorite subject: themselves. Numerous studies show that people get more pleasure from talking about themselves than they do from rewards such as money or food. Talking about ourselves triggers the same pleasure centers in the brain as food and money.

Challenge

If you feel the urge to immediately tell your story, tell yourself, "I'm not going to tell it now." Instead, focus on what the person said and ask yourself, "What did they say that I want to explore deeper?"

Complaining Is the WORST, Right? Yes. Just STOP.

"Complaining not only ruins everybody else's day, it ruins the complainer's day, too. The more we complain, the more unhappy we get." ~ Dennis Prager

We touched on this briefly before, but it bears repeating because people who complain a lot are almost universally disliked. Many of us complain without knowing we're complaining (we may think we're just stating the facts) so it pays to practice self-awareness, and begin replacing negatively skewed phrases with positivity.

In some cultures more than others, complaining is like a national sport. Actually, it is an almost universal affliction. People love to complain! It's easy, everybody does it, people say it makes them feel better and yes, it can start conversations.

We can't always solve a problem on our own, so it is okay to discuss negative things with other people in order to solve them. But, when it comes to whining about something meaningless, or you make drama out of something, then it becomes complaining, which is pointless and annoying.

This does not mean you should never say anything negative. Complaining is *not* the same as talking about life problems constructively with the intention of venting your frustrations while solving the problem. Complaining is done just for the sake of, well, complaining; often about something trivial, without necessarily wanting an answer or a solution.

Complaining: "I can't believe they don't have valet parking here! It is such a busy area and finding parking is impossible."
Talking about life problems: "I remember a friend saying it is hard to find parking around that restaurant so let's leave early and enjoy a good walk before we stuff ourselves silly."

Complaining: "My car is falling apart, and my mechanic is an idiot who can't fix anything." **Talking about life problems:** "My car keeps having problems with (x) and my mechanic can't seem to find the problem. Can you recommend anyone?"

Complaining: "It always rains on my days off from work!"
Talking about life problems: "It looks like I made a less than ideal choice of hobbies to do in our climate. Do you have anything you enjoy doing that isn't affected by the weather?"

Challenge

The trouble with negativity is that it is a learned behavior because it gets attention (even if the attention is negative) and it very quickly becomes a habit. Here's how to let it go forever:
1. If what you are talking about is unimportant, let it go. Don't even mention it or if you do, put a positive spin on it.
2. If what you are talking about is important, talk about it with the intent of finding a solution.

Don't Be a Gossip

"Save your skin from the corrosive acids from the mouths of toxic people. Someone who just helped you to speak evil about another person can later help another person to speak evil about you." ~ Israelmore Ayivor

If you've ever heard someone saying something unkind or downright nasty about someone who's not present, you may agree with their assessment of the person... but at the same time, you also know that they are just as likely to be completely two-faced and spreading negativity about you behind your back. Gossips are not trustworthy, and they are not likable.

Any time you complain about someone, judge them, blame them, or criticize them, think of it as a form of gossip. Chances are always good that this information will get back to them.

Complaining, judging, blaming, and criticizing are closely related and they are all obnoxious. There's nothing wrong with pointing out a problem with an individual, but if it is done just for the sake of elevating yourself above them, and it is done behind their back, then this is the opposite of being likable and you come to be seen as depressing and cynical.

Challenge

Whenever you hear gossip about someone, turn the conversation around immediately by saying something nice about the person. If you don't know the person, it is okay to say that you don't know the person and would prefer to make up your own mind about them. If the gossiper is insulted... well, this person is not someone you want to be friends with anyway. You can be 100% certain that whoever speaks badly about others behind their backs, will speak badly about you behind yours! Ultimately, anyone else listening in will respect you for standing up for the person being gossiped about.

Don't Get on the Negativity Train

"Watch out for the joy-stealers: gossip, criticism, complaining, fault finding, and a negative, judgmental attitude." ~ Joyce Meyer

If a group of people are mutually complaining, gossiping, judging, or blaming, it does not mean you have to chime in with your own negativity. There is no reason to join the grumpy parade! None of these are productive. If people aren't constructively seeking a solution, don't feel obligated to join in their negativity.

Remember: the words you say will *always* become tied to how other people see you!

Challenge

Become known for being the one to change the negativity; otherwise, it will feed on itself. Disrupt their downward spiral by saying something funny or positive.

Chapter 8: Make People Feel Important, Valued, and Respected

It's Not About You

"The greatest compliment that was ever paid me was when one asked me what I thought, and attended to my answer." ~ Henry David Thoreau

A proven way to create a bond is to take the focus off yourself and put it on the other person and make them feel that they matter.

The most important thing you can do with anyone you meet is to seek their thoughts and opinions, *without judging them.*

Here's how to make people feel good in your company.

Be Present and Attentive

"The utmost form of respect is to give sincerely of your presence." ~ Mollie Marti

Silence your phone and temporarily forget about whatever you have to do in the future. Just be here. If you are lost in thought, a million miles away from the speaker, they can tell, and the conversation will grind to a halt (and they will resent you for your inattention).

If you are constantly distracted by other people or your phone, you are basically communicating that this person isn't that important to you. Of course, they will pick up on that. Notice that likable people are fully present when they are talking to you. This is one of the most important communication skills you can develop.

<u>Challenge</u>

Whatever you are worried about, whatever is keeping your attention off the speaker, tell yourself that it can wait. You do not have to put it aside forever, just for the duration of this conversation. Just promise yourself you will get back to it as soon as you can put your attention on it.

Make It About Them: Not About You

"Interest and enthusiasm are the wellspring of continually evolving community life: they create bonds which unite us whether we are young or old, nearby or far from each other; they allow human warmth and love to be the formative forces in personal and community life."
~ Henning Hansmann

We all love to talk about ourselves. It's simply human nature. However, we all know how annoying it is to hear someone prattle on and on about themselves, as if nobody else existed. Likable people will always express genuine interest in others and make the person they are speaking with feel like they are the center of the universe.

Janelle relates a story about a date she went on. They met online, and in their initial online chats they seemed to have a lot in common and the conversation was going well. They agreed to meet for dinner, and this is where it all went downhill. She remembers, "All he talked about was himself. 100% of the time. There was not a single question about me, no sign of interest in anything about me. I remember sitting there in silence trying to be polite and wondering when he would shut up and ask me *one single question* about me. As the evening dragged on, I remember thinking, 'If you are so fascinating why don't you go date yourself?' and the first date turned into the last date."

Do share ideas and information when the time is right but do your best to naturally steer the conversation back to them. Unless it is your wedding day or you are standing on the podium with a medal around your neck, you should not be the center of attention if you want people to genuinely like you.

Be a friend they can approach to share their day and their worries… without circling around to make the conversation about you. If it IS about you, for example about an accomplishment or experience you had, that's fine! But don't overdo it.

Never take over a conversation to make it about you.

Making the conversation about the other person is one of those "art of conversation" skills that will make you instantly likable.

Challenge

Everyone is the center of their own universe: there's no denying that. We are each our own favorite topics of conversation… so taking the time to listen to someone's stories can be extremely meaningful to them.

Offer Non-Judgmental Validation

"A real conversation always contains an invitation. You are inviting another person to reveal herself or himself to you, to tell you who they are or what they want." ~ David Whyte

The single most important thing about conversation is non-judgmental validation or seeking someone else's ideas and opinions without judging them.

It can be hard to avoid judging someone but try. Nobody likes to be judged, including you.

Seeking thoughts and opinions without judging does not mean you agree with their point of view. It's that you respect that other people see life differently and you validate that everyone has a right to their perspective.

As soon as you hear something that you do not necessarily agree with or understand, instead of judging it, immediately show interest. Seek to *learn… to open your mind…* and let them continue talking about their favorite subject: themselves.

Challenge

When someone starts to share their thoughts and opinions, let them speak and do not interrupt or judge them. If you find yourself judging, ask questions that help you understand.

Ask for More: "I Would Love to Hear About…"

"The true secret of happiness lies in taking a genuine interest in all the details of daily life." ~ William Morris

Sometimes, we meet people that we initially think are boring or we feel we have nothing in common. Often, they are just reserved and waiting for the right time to share.

Sometimes, we feel that a topic is too boring to make good conversation, but the person you are with thinks it is interesting. One way to become instantly likable is to exhibit curiosity. Get them talking about their passions and interests—not in an interrogative way but rather, gently with something like "I would love to hear about…".

Once you get someone talking about a topic that lights them up inside, you will see them come alive. Your interest in their passion will create a bond between you. They will instinctively feel that you would support them in achieving their dreams rather than judging them: and what better feeling is there, than to know you are not being judged?

Challenge

Take the attitude of a child who is curious about everything… even topics you are not interested in. You just never know when a topic could spark fascination because of a connection to something you are interested in!

Be Genuinely Complimentary

"Everyone needs to know how to accept compliments and say thank you." ~ Matt Czuchry

Elevate people with genuine praise. Never compliment or praise someone just to be liked.

People immediately spot insincere compliments so heed the old adage, "if you don't have anything nice to say, don't say anything." Avoid filling space with insincere compliments; not because the person won't want to hear you say something (falsely) complimentary even if it strokes their ego… but because you will be perceived as insincere.

<u>Challenge</u>

Many people are just as bad at giving compliments as they are at receiving compliments. The next time you have a reason to give a compliment, do it, especially if it is unexpected.

Speak Kindly and Respectfully About Everyone

"Be modest, be respectful of others, try to understand." ~ Lakhdar Brahimi

Always speak kindly and respectfully about *everyone*, even people you dislike or disagree with strongly. Showing respect for people (and especially those we disagree with) is a trait that likable people have developed.

Why does someone who has done awful things deserve any respect at all? Most people, most of the time, don't do truly horrific things. They may act and speak thoughtlessly and unkindly, but it is important to understand that when someone acts or speaks hurtfully, it comes from very deep pain within them. This does not excuse the behavior, of course; but being compassionate to their pain can help you understand them just a little better.

One of the most important elements of becoming a likable person is this:

Whatever you say has a powerful boomerang effect. Whatever words you put out there, will have less to do with the person you are speaking about than with you; and *you will be remembered for those words.*

People use the adjectives you use to describe others as a measure of your personality. In other words, whatever you say about other people influences how people see you.

- If you express jealousy at someone's good looks or wealth, you will be perceived as jealous.
- If you compliment people and celebrate their successes, you will be seen as someone who's a genuinely good person who wants to see everyone thrive, even competitors.
- If you describe a mutual friend as kind and nurturing, the listener will associate those traits with you as well!
- When you are gossiping about people behind their backs, the negative qualities you describe will stick to you like glue and that's how people will perceive you.
- If you talk about how lazy people are, people may think that you judge them the same if they are having an off day and aren't performing at 100%.

Mind your words, for they will come back to you!

Challenge

Whenever a critical or judgmental phrase is about to leave your lips, challenge yourself to focus on something positive about them instead and keep the judgment silent.

Be Empathetic

"Sometimes all a person wants is an empathetic ear; all he or she needs is to talk it out. Just offering a listening ear and an understanding heart for his or her suffering can be a big comfort."
~ Roy T. Bennett

Empathy is the ability to put yourself into others' shoes and helps you to be a good listener—a sounding board where the other person can talk things out without being judged and without having you solve a problem for them. At the same time, being empathetic does not mean letting someone drag you down into their misery.

Asking open-ended questions helps you understand their point of view and what they are feeling and allows them to process their emotions. And sometimes, just being there in complete silence is all they need.

Challenge

One of the most wonderful things you can say to a friend who is going through a difficult time is: "We'll get through this together." You do not need to have all of the answers. You do not need to know "how"; just knowing that you are there can bring immense comfort to a friend. It's a gesture that will be remembered.

Never Talk Down

"When you choose to look down on something, you render yourself incapable of understanding it." ~ Stewart Stafford

When likable people explain something, they never say it in a condescending way. Even though they may know a lot more about a topic, they also realize that at one time, they were also complete beginners who knew absolutely nothing about it. They also realize that the person they are talking to probably has superior knowledge about other things.

Challenge

When explaining a concept to someone, first ask them how much they already know about it.

Don't Offer Unsolicited Advice

"There is a time to provide advice and offer an opinion, and there is a time not to. Don't be too quick to offer unsolicited advice. It certainly will not endear you to people." ~ Harvey Mackay

Likable people do not offer unsolicited advice. They avoid using the phrase "you should," no matter how expert they are on a subject. If it is clear the person needs help, likable people ask open-ended questions and listen empathetically to help the other person formulate their own solutions. They only offer ideas or solutions when advice is directly asked for.

You would be amazed at how effective asking open-ended questions can be, in supporting people in solving their problems. It positions you as a person who values what people have to say, which helps them open up even more and talk through their problems.

If asked, you could offer your experience as a way of showing that you understand. However, keep in mind that everyone's life experience is vastly different. You have no idea how they see things, what their background is, or what they feel capable of, which is why offering unsolicited advice is extremely disrespectful.

Challenge

Think about the times someone said "you should" to you, and you found it annoying and condescending. "You should" is a phrase that's pure opinion; an opinion that has nothing to do with the listener and everything to do with the speaker.

If you are tempted to offer advice, ask! Simply ask if the person would like some input. If they say yes, great. If not, just drop it.

Use Friendly Phrases

"For beautiful eyes, look for the good in others; for beautiful lips, speak only words of kindness; and for poise, walk with the knowledge that you are never alone." ~ Audrey Hepburn

There are a few proven phrases that instantly boost your likability. Sprinkle them throughout your conversation—and make note of when people say them to you so you can see how good they make you feel:

- How are you feeling?
- I'm so glad we're doing this together!
- You are looking well.
- I appreciate you.
- What are your plans for (x)?
- Thank you.
- You look happy.
- How can I help?
- I understand.
- I believe in you!
- I enjoyed doing (x) with you.
- Congratulations!
- Sure, let's try that!
- You can do it!
- You are welcome.
- You are awesome!
- I'm so impressed!
- I don't know but I'll find out.
- You did really well!
- I enjoy your company.
- I am so thankful to know you.
- What do you think about …?
- I'm sorry.
- I miss you.
- We'll get through this together.

- I'm here for you.
- I feel you.
- This, too, shall pass.

Challenge

Think about a phrase someone said that made you feel better during a difficult time; and a phrase someone said that made you feel even better when you were already happy.

Become a Great Listener

"We are far more revealing by the questions we ask than the answers we give. Answer briefly to sense where their questions are heading." ~ Kare Anderson

There's an art to listening, and most people get it wrong especially in first meetings. Why else would remembering people's names be such a struggle?

Most people think they are good listeners. We tend to think that good listening means:
- Not talking or interrupting when others are speaking
- Being able to repeat what people say ("So let me make sure I understand, you said...")
- Letting them know you are listening through sounds ("MM-hmm"), nods, and facial expressions

However, there's much more to being the kind of listener that encourages people to open up and keep talking.

Good Listening is Part of an Active Two-Way Dialogue

"If there is no communication then there is no respect. If there is no respect, then there is no caring. If there is no caring, then there is no understanding. If there is no understanding, then there is no compassion. If there is no compassion, then there is no empathy. If there is no empathy, then there is no forgiveness. If there is no forgiveness, then there is no kindness. If there is no kindness, then there is no honesty. If there is no honesty, then there is no love. If there is no love, then God doesn't reside there. If God doesn't reside there, then there is no peace. If there is no peace, then there is no happiness. If there is no happiness—then there IS CONFLICT BECAUSE THERE IS NO COMMUNICATION!" ~ Shannon L. Alder

Have you ever been in a situation where you are speaking, the other person is nodding, and then you ask them a question and it becomes clear that they weren't listening at all?

Even if a particular conversation isn't the most exciting time in your life, remind yourself that you want to be heard; so extend the same courtesy to the speaker.

Challenge

Instead of sitting there nodding quietly (which does not mean you are listening), wait for the speaker to finish and ask a question. Thought-provoking questions promote insight and discovery and tell the speaker that not only are you listening, but that you are listening deeply enough to want more information. The focus is on the speaker, not on you.

Good Listening is Cooperative, Not Competitive

"The aim of argument, or of discussion, should not be victory, but progress." ~ Joseph Joubert

Poor listeners tend to be seen as competitive, more interested in winning an argument than coming to an understanding. You will notice that when people are "competitive listeners" they use their silence (while the other person is speaking) to formulate their response, to point out errors in logic or reasoning, or to let their emotions build. They never actually take the time to understand the speaker's point of view.

Challenge

Develop the likable trait of cooperative listening by becoming curious about what the other person is saying, and why. There can be no understanding without curious listening.

Good Listening is Safe

"When we fear what other people think about us, we are frequently more focused on 'being interesting' and less focused on 'taking an interest.' That's why many people talk a great deal when they are anxious and why many people never feel heard. If both people and conversation are trying to be interesting, there is no one left to genuinely listen." ~ John Yokoyama

There will be plenty of times where you are speaking with someone you disagree with strongly. While it can be hard to suspend judgment and simply listen openly to what they are saying, it is one of the most likable traits you can develop. Imagine you are saying something and the person you are speaking to instantly starts criticizing your point of view. Are you likely to continue? Probably not, because you feel attacked.

This is common in romantic relationships but applies to all human interactions: if someone asks you why you held off on telling them about a problem, how likely are you to tell them that every time you share a problem the other person acts defensively, and you get attacked or criticized?

Being likable means making people feel safe in talking to you. They never have to wonder whether you are going to attack them for their ideas. They feel:
- Safe expressing themselves fully and authentically
- Safe sharing personal fears and insecurities
- Safe expressing dissatisfaction with something the listener said or did
- Safe having a conversation about a difficult subject without it escalating
- Safe to know they won't be yelled at, shamed, blamed, insulted, or rejected

Even if you disagree, make it a point to seek understanding. Good listeners make the speaker feel important, valued, and respected; they create a safe space where differences and problems can be discussed openly without fear of backlash.

Here's how to create a safe environment for people to talk to you.

- Listen non-defensively with the intent to understand. Even if you do not agree with the other person's feelings, they have a right to them, and you can still practice validation: recognizing that everyone has a right to see things the way they see them.

- Let go of the labels you've assigned to the person (the human brain, if you remember, flash-processes information about others; and a negative first impression can directly influence how empathetic you are and whether you truly listen to them or not).

- Practice good listening body language: don't roll your eyes, turn your back, fold your arms, sigh, make negative facial expressions, or walk away. Good listening body language means mirroring them and also encouraging them with comfortable eye contact, facing the person, attentive facial expressions, and where appropriate, light physical touch.

- Thank them for sharing! This means a lot to the speaker because it communicates trust: no matter how difficult the subject, you trust one another enough to have the conversation in the first place. The speaker is feeling vulnerable, and the best gift you can give is to try to understand them rather than attacking them.

Challenge

Put yourself in the shoes of someone who wants to share a difficult subject: a subject that you are afraid or ashamed to talk about. What would you like the listener to say or do, to encourage you to share?

Good Listening Is a Learning Experience

"She recognized that that is how friendships begin: one person reveals a moment of strangeness, and the other person decides just to listen and not exploit it." ~ Meg Wolitzer

Good listening means leaving your ego at the door and opening your mind. Think of listening as a learning experience. When you are listening, you are literally learning to see things from the speaker's point of view.

Whatever your differences, if you take this with the attitude of fascination, you will be more likely to come to an understanding of the speaker's point of view, and potentially an amicable resolution to a conflict.

Listening does not mean you have nothing to say; it means you respect the speaker enough to understand them and not start thinking about how you can jump in with your own story the moment they start talking.

In other words: being a good listener does NOT mean being a sponge.

Instead, good listening is more like a wall in a tennis court, where you can bounce ideas off the listener and let your questions (your active participation) energize, clarify, and support the speaker in solving a problem.

Even if there's no problem to discuss, good listening promotes the sharing of ideas (for example, where to go on vacation, how to remodel a kitchen, etc.).

Not every conversation requires deep listening. Or does it? Even a casual encounter could lead to a lifelong friendship, *if* you present yourself as a good listener.

Challenge

Challenge yourself to learn one new thing every time you have a discussion with someone.

Build Emotional Intimacy

"It has been my experience that if we make the effort to listen to people when we meet them, and work to get to know them a little, it is then easy to find something likeable in practically anyone." ~ Bryant H. McGill

Likable people make the effort to connect. Even if it may seem there's no common ground, likable people understand that common ground always appears, even if it's with a little digging. Building emotional intimacy begins with open listening, a genuine interest in someone, and a desire to know more. Here are some additional tactics for building emotional intimacy.

Share Secrets

"Secrets make life more interesting. You can be in a crowded room with someone and touch them without touching, just with a look, because they know a part of you no one else knows. And whenever you are with them, the two of you are alone, because they see the you no one else can." ~ Mohsin Hamid

Likable people create emotional intimacy by sharing secrets. Self-disclosure is just as vulnerable as the physical act of adopting an open stance. Sharing information puts the other person at ease and makes them more likely to reciprocate. Just as importantly, keeping a secret is an essential part of being a good friend.

Of course, you do not have to divulge everything about your whole life and share all of your sordid stories and mistakes in the first few meetings (the other person would probably feel as though you are treating them like a psychiatrist).

There are different levels of emotional intimacy. For example, sharing a story of an affair with a new coworker is not appropriate. Let the situation dictate the level of emotional intimacy. You could share a story of time you were humbled by a mistake you made.

Challenge

Think about a time someone shared a secret with you, and how it brought you closer. Or, if you do not have personal experience with this, think about how getting something off your chest felt like a big release because you alone did not have to bear the burden anymore.

Don't Be Afraid to Be Human: Admit Your Mistakes

"Admitting a mistake is not a weakness; on the contrary, it shows an openness of your heart. It takes guts to say sorry. Only a strong and well-balanced individual with clarity of mind can do so effortlessly. Taking responsibility for your actions requires and develops your self-control. You become your own person." ~ Vishwas Chavan

The Pratfall Effect states that people will like you more after you have made a mistake, but only if they initially believe you to be competent. In other words, they are more likely to identify with someone who's accomplished but is still a human and makes mistakes. They are less likely to identify with a bumbling idiot or a perfectionist who never shows flaws.

A University of Texas study revealed that simple mistakes can affect perceived attraction. Male participants were asked to listen to recordings of people (actors) taking a quiz. The actors were told to "take the quiz" and either perform well or poorly; they were also instructed to either spill their coffee after they finished the quiz, or not spill it. People who performed well on the quiz but spilled coffee at the end were more favorably perceived. Both the actors who did well on the quiz and did not spill coffee, and those who did not do well and spilled their coffee, were less favorably rated on likability.

The takeaway from this study is that revealing that you aren't perfect makes you more relatable and vulnerable as long as you are generally seen as competent.

"Remember, you have been criticizing yourself for years and it hasn't worked. Try approving of yourself and see what happens." ~ Louise L. Hay

People do not want to be around boastful individuals who are always competing for supremacy (one-upmanship); but they will also walk away from people who are always putting themselves down. People like to be around inspiring people, not downers.

You don't even have to share anything personal early in the relationship. But it is a way to strengthen a bond; so share, in moderation, over time and you will find that if you share something emotional, the relationship is more likely to move forward than if you don't. Take the risk. Expose your heart!

But… never throw yourself under the bus. Do not admit to every single flaw and weakness. We all have aspects of ourselves that need work; so don't overdo it, and don't make yourself the center of attention by being a victim of your flaws (essentially, asking for attention and pity).

Above all, do not make a conversation all about you! You can share a more intimate piece of information, and get more involved in their story when they reciprocate.

Challenge

Not everyone feels comfortable sharing more personal details of their lives so do not expect them to automatically reciprocate. Read the situation and share a piece of information about yourself they would not necessarily figure out on their own. It may encourage them to share something about themselves; but if they hold back in sharing, it's okay. Keep the conversation going on another topic.

Be Open-Minded

"Until the mind is open, the heart stays closed. The open mind is the key to the open heart." ~ Byron Katie

Most of us like to think we're open-minded but the truth is, we are all closed-minded to some degree. We believe XYZ about practically everything we know, and most of us do not like to have our beliefs challenged.

It's safe to say that we are open-minded *only* to ideas that fit within our own particular belief system. It's not that we choose to be closed-minded; we all (as adults) come with a robust belief system, and people generally dislike change.

There are people who will change their minds when presented with facts; and then there are those who refuse to change, insisting that "this is the way things are which means the information you are presenting is wrong." While these people are closed off to differing opinions and beliefs, does not mean you have to be.

Challenge

In conversations where you disagree, make a point of exploring their points of view. Be curious. Ask open-ended questions. Ask them why they believe something, in a way that's not threatening. Something like, "Wow, I never thought about it that way. Did you have an experience that proved this?"

Find Common Ground

"No matter what message you are about to deliver somewhere, whether it is holding out a hand of friendship, or making clear that you disapprove of something, is the fact that the person sitting across the table is a human being, so the goal is to always establish common ground." ~ Madeleine Albright

The similarity-attraction effect states that people are more attracted to those who are similar to them and share similar beliefs. This is an evolutionary trait that has stood the test of time. One study measured subjects' attitudes on sensitive topics (including politics and sex), and then put them in a shared living situation. At the end of the stay with their new housemates, the subjects were asked to evaluate their housemates: as predicted, they reported liking the housemates that held shared similar attitudes and values about those particular topics.

This does not mean that you have to compromise your beliefs or even change your mind in order to be liked. In fact, don't ever change just to fit in! Even if people initially gravitate toward those with whom they share values and attitudes on certain topics, you can find plenty of common ground outside of these topics.

"Embrace a diversity of ideas. Embrace the fact that you can disagree with people and not be disagreeable. Embrace the fact that you can find common ground—if you disagree on nine out of ten things, but can find common ground on that tenth, maybe you can make progress. If you can find common ground, you can accomplish great things." ~ David Boies

So what happens if you meet someone with views that are completely opposite to yours? Does this mean you can't be friends? No! Of course, you could stick to generic topics and avoid the emotional topics although eventually these will come out as the friendship grows, but by then the bond should be strong enough that differences will not matter, and you can talk respectfully and openly about sensitive topics.

What can you do if the other person is vehemently holding their ground on a topic and does not seem to be open to learning about your point of view? Try this:

- Stop trying to explain your point of view and put your emphasis on trying to understand their point of view. If they feel heard, they are more likely to be more open to your perspective. But ultimately a conversation is not about changing their opinion or changing yours, it is about coming to a mutual understanding. You can still disagree, but continue to remain friends.

- Put more emphasis on shared values. Look for the common ground instead of pointing out the differences. This can quickly disarm someone who is already on the defensive: by pointing out shared values, you are "on their team."

- Be respectful of their point of view. A phrase such as, "Wow, I never saw it from that perspective. I really appreciate you sharing that with me," is non-committal yet respectful. They haven't converted you to their point of view and you haven't converted them either, but at least you are showing consideration for them.

A good conversation is not about you winning an argument, it is about creating common ground that could, despite your differences, be enough to forge a friendship based on other factors.

The main takeaway from this chapter is that people love to talk about themselves… so let them! Your curiosity about them will spark their curiosity about you.

Challenge

Notice that likable people may be very committed to their point of view, but they are also willing to understand differences.

Think about a time when you strongly disagreed with someone, and neither of you would budge on your opinion. What was the outcome? If you could go back in time, what could you have asked to better understand their point of view?

Chapter 9: Act Like a Friend

Be the Person Everybody Wants to Befriend

"Listen carefully, be transparent, be responsive, be authentic, tell great stories—the qualities that would make you the hotshot at a party." ~ Dave Kerpen

So far, you've learned what likability isn't, what it is, focusing on making just one connection at a time, first impressions and how to break the ice with some great conversation-starters, the art of conversation, and how to make people feel good.

This is *most* of what you need to know in order to become someone that people want to be friends with.

I encourage you to practice these methods outlined in each chapter every single day until they become second nature: until you don't have to think about your body language, smiling, opening lines, how to listen, and so on. Practice these techniques until they are as much a part of you as the favorite story you like to tell, which is basically told in exactly the same way as the time before, and the time before that… in this way, you will become a person that naturally attracts others and easily makes new friends.

Always Be Kind

"Constant kindness can accomplish much. As the sun makes ice melt, kindness causes misunderstanding, mistrust, and hostility to evaporate." ~ Albert Schweitzer

Being kind means you are compassionate, empathetic, and willing to help. However, likable people have firm boundaries. They help when they can, and they say no when they can't and someone else could step in. But because they are so kind, people don't take their "no" personally.

Challenge

Think about the last time you performed a "random act of kindness" no matter how small. How did it make you feel? How did it make the other person feel (if you know the outcome)? Simple acts of kindness, where you make a small extra effort to make someone's life just a little bit easier, are the hallmarks of likable people.

Go with the Flow

"Life is either a grand adventure, or nothing at all." ~ Helen Keller

When you think about it, going with the flow means embracing adventure. You control what you can, and when it comes to things you can't control, you just relax and let things unfold. This is a much more likable trait than the micromanager/perfectionist/control freak who has to have things a particular way or they become stressed and miserable.

Going with the flow does not mean constantly compromising on what you want just to fit in and be accepted. It means not being so rigid about getting your way or expecting a situation to work out exactly as you had imagined. Most of the time, life throws us monkey wrenches anyway, so things rarely work out like we expect. Don't stress about it. Laugh it off and enjoy the ride.

Likable people know how to let go of control, adapt, and pivot. They can see the humor in a situation and know how to lighten the mood even if nothing is going their way. And most of all, they are not rigid about how things "should" be because they are open to novel approaches. It's not "my way or the highway," it is more like "I'm curious to see how you do things."

Develop a lighthearted attitude. Think about a situation in the past where you let a situation dictate your mood (we've all been there). How likable were you in that moment? It's not enough to only be likable when the skies are blue, the sun is shining, and everything is going well. A change in attitude is all it takes.

How to Go with the Flow

"If it is meant for you, it will come to you. It will find you and reach you. So, don't despair when, despite your best intention and effort, something does not happen the way you envisioned it and planned it. Take it easy. Of course, you have every right to have an intention, put forth a plan and execute it, but you have no right to insist that just because you did all that you must get what you want. The outcomes are never in your hand. The idea that you deserve something is what you have grown within you. So, drop that idea. Just do your bit, and do it well, in any situation. And leave the results, the outcomes, to Life. If you must get it, you will. When you do, be grateful for Life's compassion. When you don't, be accepting of Life's verdict." ~ AVIS Viswanathan

In any given situation, ask yourself: *So, what if things don't work out the way I envisioned? What if they work out better?*

It's true, you might not get what you want. It's true, things might be difficult or painful. But sometimes, what is perceived as a failure to achieve a specific goal, could turn into the most wonderful, most serendipitous of "scenic detours" that takes you in a direction you would never have anticipated, where you meet amazing new people and have incredible experiences.

Choose to let go sometimes and enjoy the "scenic detour." This makes you instantly likable. Nobody likes to be around downers who complain about how awful things are when they don't go perfectly according to plan (meaning, "their" plan).

Challenge

The next time you are faced with a situation *not* going exactly as you planned, let go. Something came up, and now you are faced with a choice. You can either hold on to "your way" with all your might and create a lot of tension… or you can let go, follow someone else's idea, and see what happens. Try letting go. It can open you up to an experience you would otherwise never have.

Drop the Ego

"Your ego is your self-image created by thought. It's your social mask requiring validation because it lives in fear of losing its sense of identity." ~ Thibaut

How does ego show up to prevent you from making friends?

Let's say you are a server at a restaurant. Your customers ask for menu suggestions and wine pairings. You give your best, most enticing descriptions of your favorite dishes and several wines that would make an exquisite combination. They nod politely, and then proceed to order something else. Since you put so much effort into your presentation, you feel hurt, and inside, you go on the defensive. You just don't care about their experiences as much now that they have shot down your suggestions. During their stay, you aren't as attentive or friendly as you could be, and as a result, your tip is not great either. You go home with a bad taste in your mouth about how most people are entitled jerks.

Where did these feelings come from? Their rejection of your suggestions made you feel invalidated: like your opinion—especially since it was asked for—doesn't matter. As a result, you feel rejected.

As a human being, you want validation, and you don't want rejection (this is universal, not just "you"), and we have all felt the sting of rejection.

However, here's where the ego gets in the way. Were *you* actually rejected? Or were your *suggestions* rejected? Of course, your customers did not reject you personally. It's just your perception of things that made you think that they rejected you, and you in turn rejected them by retaliating with poor service.

Let's look at another example. You are invited to a party where you don't know anyone except the person who invited you. Let's say you are a passionate road biker, and your friend told you that there would be other cyclists there. When you show up, the conversation immediately circles around to mountain biking, and the minute you mention you're a road cyclist, the group expresses the distaste that many mountain bikers have against "uptight" road cyclists ("roadies"). Your hackles immediately go up because you feel that you are personally being attacked. The initial bond (a love of bicycles) is broken because where you initially felt like part of a tribe, you now feel like an unwanted outsider who is being sharply judged. You make your way back to your friend, make up an excuse that you don't feel well, and go home sullen, angry, and hating all mountain bikers (because they clearly hate you).

Now, because of this isolated incident, you have put up a barrier against mountain bikers, and therefore, thanks to your ego, you have closed off any chance of developing a friendship with anyone at the party.

What is the ego, exactly, and why do likable people know how to drop it?

The ego is our sense that we are separate from everything and everyone around us. It is our "I am." The ego is tied to feelings of self-importance, often accompanied by feelings of superiority and pride. Everyone has ego; I do, you do, we all do. Ego isn't bad per se, but unchecked, it can prevent friendships from developing, and make you unlikable.

We tend to think of the ego as a superiority complex where someone:
- Always thinks they are right (and everyone else is wrong)
- Never allows themselves to be seen as flawed or vulnerable
- Like to be seen as superior, on a pedestal above others
- Likes to triumph over others

"But I'm not like that," you protest. And rightly so! This dense, rigid ego isn't the only thing meant by ego. It's that sense of "I" (separation from others) that is constantly vulnerable to attack, always on guard. Really, it's a sense of self-preservation.

However, it's the sense of separation that causes trouble. We are constantly assessing life (and other people) in terms of how they may be threatening us, or how they may be helping us. The same danger signals we perceive when we're in physical danger are present when we feel threatened emotionally: when our self-image is threatened.

When someone tells you, "You are awful at your job," they are not threatening your life, but they are definitely threatening your self-esteem. As a result, you go into fight-or-flight mode and effectively slam the door on any kind of relationship with this person. The same instinctive defensive reaction occurs when your menu suggestions are rejected, or you hear that your fellow road cyclists are uptight and arrogant jerks.

Here's how to drop the ego.

Let's go back to the first example: the server. Instead of getting into a huff because your party rejected your suggestion, you could just recognize that they simply don't like the same kinds of food that you can't live without. Not everyone likes steak. Not everyone likes tofu. And it's all good. You may not like their suggestions either... And even though it was your job to suggest something, *did you even ask what types of food they like, before suggesting menu items that would appeal to them?*

Let's go back to the second example: this group of mountain bikers doesn't like roadies. Instead of letting it rest there, *did you ever give them a chance to explain why they don't like road bikers?* Did you show any interest in their experiences that could have contributed to their perception of roadies?

Asking questions and getting into someone's "why" is the gist of how to master the ego, and let things go rather than letting them escalate.

There will be many, many situations where you may feel personally attacked, but the mark of a likable person is to allow the discussion to go deeper into the "why" of someone's opinion.

Simply asking questions can help remove imaginary blocks between people: blocks that are based on faulty interpretations like in the examples above.

The ego makes itself heard anytime you go on the defensive when you feel that you are being attacked. Instead, make an effort to hear them out instead of automatically defending yourself.

Also try these two methods of dropping the ego:

1. Listen deeply to everyone, because you never know where the next brilliant solution will come from. If you are a CEO, listen to the janitor. If you are an expert, listen to the beginner. If you feel that you are superior to someone and their ideas aren't worth considering or that you can't learn anything from them, you are acting out of ego. In this way, ego closes you off to learning and growing; and it closes you off to meaningful relationships.

2. Do not correct people or tell them they are wrong. Even if you vehemently disagree with someone, correcting them and telling them they are wrong makes you instantly unlikable. When you hear something you disagree with, your brain's logical centers shut down and your brain prepares for a fight.

Nobody likes to be proven wrong (this is a trait of the ego); however, if you stop looking at things as "right or wrong" and instead start seeing things as entirely dependent on personal perspective, then you can more easily come to an understanding and mutual agreement.

Imagine yourself standing in front of an abstract statue. Imagine there's a circle of people around the statue. Each person sees something different. You see a man climbing a ladder. The person just a few feet to your right sees a palm tree and a monkey. You both "know" that what you see is right. Even just an arm's width apart, your perspectives are different and vice-versa. And you are both right. What can you do to better understand what they see, so you can understand why they disagree with you so vehemently? Ask questions. Listen. And learn.

Challenge

Think about a situation where you felt attacked, yet did not give the "attacker" a chance to explain their position; and if they did explain their position, did you still see it as "wrong"? Situations like this can help you become more self-aware of when your ego is getting in the way of your likability.

Be Inclusive

"Remember what it was like to be excluded so that you can help build a community where everyone is included." ~ Lisa Friedman

You may have had the experience where you are the lonely kid who nobody sat next to at lunch. The kid who got picked last for games. The kid who was never invited to parties or the prom. Or you may be one of those who sat by and watched it happen as everyone was picked except for that one poor kid. Or you are one of those who reached out to that kid and included him or her.

Likable people make an effort to include people, even (especially?) those who are painfully shy, or who have convinced themselves they are unlovable. All it takes is one small kind gesture to make someone's day.

Challenge

Whenever you see someone at a social gathering who is off by themselves, walk up and say hi. Use one of your trusted icebreakers.

Be Generous and Helpful… But Know When to Say No

"We make a living by what we get, but we make a life by what we give." ~ Winston Churchill

Likable people have a great attitude when it comes to generosity. Generous people readily offer help and any resources they can to help a fellow human being. It's actually in our nature to be generous and cooperative.

Has this ever happened to you? You committed to helping; beforehand, you feel stressed and find yourself making up excuses to back out even though you feel that saying yes would make you more likable. You end up going, all the while thinking, "What was I thinking? I don't have the time for this!" And afterward, you feel resentment. This resentment shows… and makes you far less likable than if you had said no in the first place.

Challenge

If you ever find yourself in a situation where someone asks for help, ask yourself whether you feel obligated to say yes, and why.

Try saying no kindly yet firmly. It might take a few tries until you get used to saying no (and you will have to "retrain" people who have come to expect a yes from you). But in the end, it will be worth it. you will have more time, more energy, and higher self-esteem.

There's a difference between being helpful and being a people-pleaser. If you feel that you must say yes, ask yourself *why* you feel you must say yes.

Challenge

When someone asks you for a favor, it is perfectly okay to respond by asking about details of the commitment, and saying that you need to think about it. This gives you the opportunity to consider if you can actually commit. If it is going to cause you stress, if it is going to interfere with something important you need to attend to, if it is going to cause resentment, if you feel pressured... then saying no is a much better option. And if they need an answer right away, you can say "no."

Become More Self-Aware

"To know yourself, you must sacrifice the illusion that you already do." ~ Vironika Tugaleva

You will never know everything about yourself—and especially, you will never see the full picture of how others see you, because you are a different person to each and every human being you interact with. This can be an eye-opener!

To your parents, you may be an entirely different person than to someone you go to the climbing gym with. Maybe to your parents, you are a mild disappointment because you chose not to become a doctor but rather chose the artist's way. Maybe to your climbing gym buddy, you are an inspiration who made them believe in themselves.

You're also not the same person to your siblings, lovers, bosses, neighbors, or friends. You are a different person to each one of them. Remember the example of standing around a statue and seeing different things? The statue is the same, but everyone sees it differently based on their own perspective; and in the case of people, that perspective refers to everyone's unique background that has shaped how they see the world.

What's important though, is that you can learn a lot from the feedback you get. Developing self-awareness helps you hone the skills that make you likable... because unless you know how people see you, how can you know what to fix?

Knowing that your words and actions will always impact other people, is a valuable soft skill. For example, you could hone your ability to use a filter (to pause before speaking and make sure your words aren't offensive). You could hone your ability to avoid making rash decisions or automatically reacting to anger with anger. You could hone your ability to make people feel valued instead of jumping in with your own stories.

But without feedback, you can't know what to up-level. So take criticism as an opportunity to be better; don't let your ego put up a wall. Become more likable thanks to other people's input.

Part of being self-aware involves awareness of speech. We tend to repeat the same stories and phrases often, to the point they are so ingrained we aren't even aware of them. If you are using self-deprecating speech and using your faults and weaknesses as excuses; if you act like you know everything; or if you hide and try to cover up the truth rather than owning your actions... then it will be harder for people to trust and like you.

Self-awareness begins with these steps:

1. Be aware of the words you use around others. Your words are a window into who you really are. *All of us are what we do and think.* If your words are pessimistic, that's how people will see you. What are people's reactions to what you say? This is vital (and often humbling) feedback. If you change the way you speak about problems, other people, yourself, and life in general, people will come to see you differently.

2. Be aware of the words you use when you have conversations with yourself. Internal conversations shape who you become. Don't let your conversations be one-sided monologues where you blindly believe every thought your mind comes up with. Ask yourself questions. Challenge the thoughts you have! For example, "I'm no good, nobody likes me, I'll never have any friends." This is a terrible thought to have, but if it sounds familiar, it has become your reality. The problem is that it is not a reflection of your reality, it is the *cause* of your reality. What you repeatedly tell yourself you are, you will become. Don't let one negative interaction drive all of your human interactions from that point onward!

<u>Challenge</u>

Always remember, you may not be able to control what happens, but you have 100% control over how you respond. Instead of reacting automatically, count to 10 and take some deep breaths before you respond.
- Unkind words can never be unsaid
- Unkind actions can never be undone

Think about the impression you make when you say something unkind to or about someone. Imagine these words sticking to you, becoming part of how others see you. And next time you get the urge to say something unkind, just avoid saying anything. Even in your mind, challenge yourself to find something good about the person.

Be Warm, and Then Competent

"Although Ronald Reagan was somebody I disagreed with on most ideological things, he was a friend of mine, and he was a very, very likable man. Ronald

Reagan, for instance, was maybe more able to get the very rich to do the right thing sometimes." ~ Warren Beatty

People are naturally drawn to those who can "do," but competence has to be tempered with warmth first, in order to create a strong bond.

If you are warm and friendly, people will feel that they can trust you, but they may not trust that you can solve a problem.

If you are competent with a "can do" attitude, people will respect you, but they will not necessarily like you.

The trick is to marry the two. First, display warmth, build rapport and get people onboard with a task. And then, display your competence in a humble way. If you present competence first, people may follow, but do not expect friendships to blossom because the first impression is already made. If you do it the other way—warmth first and then competence—the first impression will be one of "like."

Challenge

In any situation where you are tempted to take charge (because you know you are competent), pause first. Get to know people, get to know their ideas for solving a problem, and only then volunteer to take charge. And don't be upset if the answer is no; just show your friendliness and competence as part of a team.

A likable person seeks to work for the common good. In what capacity, really does not matter. You can make a valuable contribution in any capacity.

Do What You Need to Do, But Ask for Help if You Need It

"I used to have horrible cars that would always end up broken down on the highway. When I tried to flag someone down, nobody stopped. But if I pushed my own car, other drivers would get out and push with me. If you want help, help yourself—people like to see that." ~ Chris Rock

Likable people try their best, which is all that can be expected of anyone. It's unrealistic to expect perfection, but it is realistic to expect that people do their best. And likable people do. But, they can also freely admit that they don't know everything and can't do everything, and so they don't hesitate to ask for help when something is out of the scope of their abilities.

It's important to note that people naturally like to help others. Asking someone for help invites interaction and connection, and makes the helper feel valued.

"How" likable people ask for help is important. They use language that empowers the helper; they do not ask in a needy way, but in a way that makes the helper feel like part of a solution.

Sometimes, it is as simple as "Hey, can you help me move this box to the garage?" But when it comes to bigger life challenges, many people won't ask for help because they do not want to be a burden.

The reality is that feeling like a burden is a natural part of asking for help. We can't help but feel "less than" when we ask for help. We fear that the other person won't say yes, or that the yes will come with a lot of unwanted judgment and criticism.

But… the reality is also, that nobody can make it on their own. We need each other. And we want to help each other.

So embrace the anxiety that comes with asking for help. It's a vulnerable spot to be in! But like being vulnerable with your body language, or by sharing personal stories in conversation, vulnerability is one of those soft skills that can make you likable. Why? If you are vulnerable, you are human. You are flawed. You are real. And that's very likable, because we can all relate!

How to Ask for Help

"Don't be afraid to ask questions. Don't be afraid to ask for help when you need it. I do that every day. Asking for help isn't a sign of weakness, it is a sign of strength. It shows you have the courage to admit when you don't know something, and to learn something new." ~ Barack Obama

There are a few tips for reducing the anxiety and awkwardness that comes from asking for help.
Whenever you are in a situation where you need to ask for help (which, for many people, does not come easily), you first want to choose the right people to ask:

- Don't ask people who think you do not actually need help (they think you're being lazy).
- Don't ask people who do not believe your problem needs outside help.
- Don't ask people who offer their opinions but do not listen or help you talk it out.
- Don't ask people who lack the experience or relevant knowledge, if appropriate.

This does not mean that these people do not like you! It does not mean they would not help in other instances. It does not mean they are not willing; it could just be that they are unable. They may not have the time, strength, skills, connections, or knowledge to help you.

There are several ways to ask for help:
- Make it funny. Use humor to ask for help.
- Be clear and concise. Don't overshare (they do not need to know your life story).
- Test the waters. Outline what you are going to do, without asking for help. You can gauge pretty quickly how receptive someone is to hearing your challenge, or offering to help.

Challenge

The next time you need help but are hesitant to ask, try asking for advice instead. Sometimes, advice is all you really need; and there is a chance that the person will respond with an offer to help.

You will notice that likable people freely ask for help, not because they take advantage of people's good natures, but because they never hesitate to help when they can. It's a give and take.

See Others How They Want to Be Seen

"The sign of a beautiful person is that they always see the beauty in others." ~ Omar Suleiman

How do you want to be seen by your friends, family, the people you work with, your clients/customers, your romantic partner, your community, and the world in general? Most of us want to be seen for our talents, strengths, and contributions; not for our insecurities, faults, and weaknesses.

We all want to be seen for who we truly are. We want to feel safe, accepted, acknowledged in the eyes of others. Each one of us has a certain self-image, and that is how we want people to see us. Whether you see yourself as a rock star, as an "ordinary Joe or Jane," as a competent worker, as a creative, as an adventurer or a homebody… you want people to treat you accordingly.

Challenge

Have you ever noticed that people lavish compliments on their friends, colleagues, family, neighbors, even complete strangers… but never see the good in themselves? Partly it is about not wanting to be seen as boastful, but if you want people to see you as likable, you have to like yourself first.

The way you repeatedly talk to yourself *about* yourself influences the way that you behave; and this is what people respond to. Up-level your self-talk by talking to yourself just as you would to a close friend, whenever you are going through a challenging time.

Treat yourself like your best friend. You strive to see the best in your friends, so why not in yourself as well? People generally do not want to be around people filled with self-loathing, self-pity, or shame.

Lift Them Up in Conversation

"It's not what you are that holds you back, it's what you think you're not." ~ Denis Waitley

Likable people are great conversationalists. They will quickly pick up on how people see themselves… and elevate them. For example, if someone is trying hard to portray themselves as a successful businessperson, artist, athlete, etc. a likable person would support them in that by praising their accomplishments and offering encouragement such as:
- "I can't wait to read your book!"
- "I love seeing womenpreneurs crush it in the marketplace. I would love to hear about your products!"

- "I can't imagine what you go through in training. What do you do every day to compete at this level?"

Praise and encouragement do not mean stroking their ego (that is *not* what likable people do)! It's being genuine in your praise, but also encouraging introspection and growth with open-ended questions; in other words, gently nudging people to be greater than they are now while supporting their ideal of who they want to be.

The exception to this is if someone has very low self-esteem and is constantly putting themselves down. You don't want to encourage someone's low self-worth by agreeing with their poor self-assessment.

If you are with someone whose speech is always self-deprecating, you could become a beacon of light for them by pointing out their strengths. Sometimes, people just aren't used to hearing encouragement. One tiny seed of encouragement you plant in conversation could help this person blossom into their full potential.

Challenge

Think of how you would like people to see you, and what you would like them to say to you to make you feel good (and to motivate you to continue toward your dreams and goals). Once someone has shared their dreams with you, what can you say to let them know you support them?

Chapter 10: The Likability Bias in Business

It's Different for Men and Women

"All over the world, girls are raised to make themselves likeable, to twist themselves into shapes that suit other people. Please do not twist yourself into shapes to please. Don't do it. If someone likes that version of you, that version of you that is false and holds back, then they actually just like that twisted shape, and not you. And the world is such a gloriously multifaceted, diverse place that there are people in the world who will like you, the real you, as you are." ~ Chimamanda Ngozi Adichie

If you are a man, please do not skip this chapter. Understanding the biases that women have to cope with in business will help you avoid them... and it will make you more likable. Be sure to complete the men's challenge.

Unfortunately, being likable and being successful isn't always compatible... if you are a woman.

Numerous studies have shown that women who seek power or status are punished for it. "Prima donna." "Schoolmarm." And of course, "b***ch" are just a few of the insults hurled at women who have worked hard and sacrificed to be successful.

"I was once told that I had become too confident and that it made me less likeable. Many successful people will get this at some point, because the people who haven't followed a similar path can be threatened by someone who has and is unabashed about it." ~ Aimee Mullins

The correlation between success and likability is rooted in societal expectations: we expect men to be strong, direct, competitive, ambitious, and assertive. We expect men to be natural leaders and therefore, likable. If they are truly likable as people *and* their likability carries over into their leadership role, it is a bonus.

Success and likability are positively correlated in men, but the opposite is true in women who are expected to focus on family and community, rather than power or success.

"We have a world full of women who are unable to exhale fully because they have for so long been conditioned to fold themselves into shapes to make themselves likeable." ~ Chimamanda Ngozi Adichie

Likable women are often described as warm, modest, helpful, nurturing, and nice—the exact opposite of how we perceive leadership traits—and the minute women assert themselves and speak directly, they are suddenly seen as bossy, overly aggressive, and intimidating. Sure, they get things done, but they turn into she-dragons.

And yet, if they remain "likable" they are seen as less competent. Women are expected to be pliant, pleasant, and to take a supportive role as good wives, employees, or even business partners (the partnership is rarely equal).

Women have to deal with this bias every day in business.

"The implications of likability are long-lasting and serious. Women adjust their behavior to be likable and as a result have less power in the world. And this desire to be liked and accepted goes beyond the boardroom—it is an issue that comes up for women in their personal lives as well, especially as they become more opinionated and outspoken." ~ Jessica Valenti

All other things being equal, likability is the one trait that can hold women back in careers. In performance reviews, it is not uncommon for a woman to be told she's good (i.e., effective) but too aggressive. Men do not get this type of negative feedback; when they are aggressive, they hear, "Go get 'em, tiger!"

Often, the worst things we call successful, powerful women are extremely derogatory ("bi**ch" is the most common, and they only go downhill from there.

But what are the worst things we call men? "Girl. Bi**ch. P**sy." The worst thing you can call a woman is a woman. The worst thing you can call a man is a woman. Culturally, the ultimate insult is to be a woman and unfortunately this holds true in business as well.

However, there are things women can do to be liked *and* to be seen as competent leaders.

First, accept that things aren't going to change anytime soon. Changing stereotypes in any society is a slow and difficult process.

Both men and women need to raise awareness of this unconscious age-old bias that the more successful a woman becomes, the less she is perceived as likable by both men and women (one would hope that women support each other, but this sadly does not appear to be the case). By contrast, the more successful a man is, the higher he ranks in likability.

A Woman's Guide to Being Successful AND Remaining Likable

"As women get more powerful, they get less likable. I see women holding themselves back because of this, but if we start talking about the success-likability penalty women face, then we can do something about it." ~ Sheryl Sandberg

First, there will always be haters. There will always be people who are jealous of your success and will lash out with unkind words.

What you may not know is that headway is being made.

Successful women are finding creative ways to overcome likability bias (another term, really, for gender bias). Many executive-level women employ similar strategies overcoming the likability bias.

Women in leadership roles need to display "masculine" qualities such as being direct and assertive. But, then they risk being seen as bad people, not just bad leaders. Savvy women quickly learn to demonstrate competence in feminine ways.

If you are a woman, here's what you can do to remain likable and still rise through the ranks:

1. Find Common Ground

Knowing how to find common ground is a valuable skill to have, and it may be the only way to shift the current culture away from a gender likability bias. It could be considered a female trait, if you look at women as nurturing and cooperative. Put this to use, and you will likely find less resistance as you rise through the ranks.

Connections happen when we have things in common. Having common ground signals the brain, "I am like this person" and we tend to like people who are similar to us.

In fact, saying "I am like you" is basically saying, "I like you."

Commonality can be found in the work environment (shared goals) as well as in our personal lives. One-on-one conversations are a brilliant way to get to know each team member and chat in a relaxed manner about travel, books, movies, music, or other shared passions.

In business, finding common ground leads to more cooperation. You are thought of less as aggressive, and more as assertively moving the team toward a common goal.

The trick is finding common ground. In the chapter on communication, you will find awesome icebreakers that can spark conversations among your team.

2. Promote a Cause

When a woman entrepreneur focuses on her company's social impact, she is seen more favorably. This brilliant strategy accomplishes two things:

- It actually does good in the world (and allows the woman to do well by doing good)
- It removes the cognitive dissonance between her success as an entrepreneur and maintaining a nurturing community focus

3. Be the Mom—A TOUGH Mom

When you embrace stereotypes like being the office mom, you may think that you are reinforcing the stereotype of nurturing women. However, mothers can also be incredibly tough. Be as assertive as you would be if you were advocating for or disciplining your kids.

Never apologize for speaking up. Many women unconsciously apologize too often for things they shouldn't apologize for: "I'm sorry, but can I interject here?" (men never do that). Successful women—and mothers—never apologize for giving direction to their family. Motherhood is, by its very nature, an incredible mix of authoritativeness and warmth. If you get negative feedback such as "you are too intimidating," you can make an effort to get to know people, find common ground, and make yourself more approachable.

4. Embrace Your Femininity

One very interesting strategy often used by successful women is to be extremely feminine in appearance, to soften their assertive behavior (this may not appeal to everyone but will work for some). An overt "gender display"—such as wearing bright pink lipstick, avoiding mimicking male business attire (never wearing pantsuits)—sends a subconscious signal that you are feminine, nurturing, warm, community-minded, etc.

5. Change the Language

Change some of the language that is commonly used in your workplace: "hunting" new clients could become "nurturing relationships" and "crushing the competition" could be "growing our customer base." It's subtle things like this that bring a touch of feminine to the workplace, and slowly help remove the invisible ladder that men (especially white men) have access to.

If someone says they don't like how you "bragged" about your accomplishments or strengths, you could reply with: "Can you tell me the difference between bragging and being confident? Please help me understand why you think I'm bragging." Will this make you likable? Perhaps not with this person but if anyone else is present, it will help with awareness of how differently men and women are perceived.

6. Don't Let It Be Okay

As I mentioned, there will always be haters so be as assertive as comes naturally to you. You may find that you are getting a lot of backlash for behaving as assertively as is natural for you—but you can always speak up and let people know what they are doing (remember, this is a social complex, an unconscious bias that we all grew up with). When people are asked to justify their position, it can help reduce an unconscious bias in decision-making.

- Write what you want to write.
- Say what you want to say.
- Do not apologize for speaking up or sharing ideas.
- Do not filter everything you say with "Oh, I hope I won't hurt anyone's feelings. I hope they like me!"
- Advocate for other women.

You may not win any likability points as a woman for speaking up against likability bias, but maybe the sacrifice is worth it as you pave the way for younger women who will follow in your footsteps.

Challenge for Men

There are things you can do as a man to confront bias, challenge stereotypes, and support women in your organization so that likability and success can become less tied to gender.

1. Challenge the speaker. If someone calls a woman "bossy" or the b-word, ask for a specific example of what she did or said and then confront them with, "Would you call a man that if he did or said the same thing?" If you ever have the urge to use those terms when describing a female boss, ask yourself the same question.

2. Give fair performance evaluations and feedback. Women are more likely to be hired and promoted based on what they have already accomplished, while men are more likely to be hired and promoted based on their potential. Clearly define "excellent performance" and make sure performance goals are defined, understood, and measurable. Give skills-based performance reviews

rather than style-based performance reviews (a common problem when evaluating men vs. women).

3. Give credit where it is due. Women are often given less credit for successful outcomes and blamed more for failure. Give women the credit they deserve.

4. Emphasize accomplishments when introducing female teammates.

5. Encourage women to go for it. Push back when a woman says she isn't ready or unqualified for an opportunity, and push back even harder when others say that about a woman simply based on her gender.

6. Encourage women to sit near the head of the table in meetings. Ask women to contribute. If a woman is interrupted, insist that she be allowed to finish speaking.

7. Be aware of "stolen ideas" and acknowledge when ideas were presented and/or developed by women.

8. Ask men to take meeting notes, train new hires, and otherwise do more of the "office housework."

9. Support working moms by supporting dads too. Being a working mom generates assumptions that she's less committed to her career. Encourage your company to adopt equal family leave (paternity leave as well as maternity leave), to help foster the idea that both parents should take equal responsibility in raising their kids rather than one parent making career sacrifices.

Lead by Example

"Even in a crowded room, likable leaders make people feel like they are having a one-on-one conversation, as if they are the only person in the room that matters. And, for that moment, they are. Likable leaders communicate on a very personal, emotional level." ~ Travis Bradberry

You do not have to consider yourself a natural leader, to be a leader. You may end up in a leadership role just because you are a likable person who intuitively knows how to motivate a team. Or, you may be in a supportive role. Either way, if you motivate someone to action, you are automatically a leader.

"If you want to be a leader whom people follow with absolute conviction, you have to be a likable leader. Tyrants and curmudgeons with brilliant vision can command a reluctant following for a time, but it never lasts. They burn people out before they ever get to see what anyone is truly capable of." ~ Travis Bradberry

Always lead by example, never "do as I say, not do as I do." Never use threats to force people to do your bidding. Instead, elevate people. Bring out the best in people and galvanize them toward a common goal.

"Likable leaders truly believe that everyone, regardless of rank or ability, is worth their time and attention. They make everyone feel valuable because they believe that everyone is valuable." ~ Travis Bradberry

If you are a leader, solicit ideas from your team. This is a leadership trait that is not often discussed, largely because leaders often develop an ego. You would be surprised at how many amazing ideas come from people who aren't in roles you would normally expect innovative solutions from: janitors, administrative assistants, assembly line workers, HR personnel, etc. Always remember, there's more than one perspective and if you solicit ideas from your entire team, you not only make people feel valued, but you could spark some incredible genius-level ideas.

Just as importantly, support people who are struggling in their roles. Think about some of the conversation and listening skills you can apply with someone who isn't performing up to expectations:
- Listen deeply to their concerns.
- Help them believe in themselves.
- Motivate them by helping them see the value they contribute.
- Solicit their opinions, especially if your views are vastly different.

Leadership is about supporting people in dropping barriers and encouraging cooperation.

"Few things kill likeability as quickly as arrogance. Likable leaders don't act as though they are better than you because they don't think that they are better than you. Rather than being a source of prestige, they see their leadership position as bringing them additional accountability for serving those who follow them." ~ Travis Bradberry

Building a solid team of people *who know that you care*, is actually one of those hidden leadership traits that can help you climb through the ranks at work.

Team Challenge

If you are a leader, you can encourage bonding among a mixed-gender team with this exercise:

Ask your teammates to write down how they are alike (to find common ground). One by one, have each person share what they wrote. Studies show that when you focus on similarities, you are more likely to pay attention to them and care about them more.

Chapter 11: Being You: Awesome, Likable You

Be Interesting (Even if You Don't Think You Are Interesting)

"This is the Law of Likability: The real you is the best you." ~ Michelle Tillis Lederman

Most of us don't think we are very interesting, or that we live interesting lives. We believe that unless we have epic adventures or harrowing near-death escapes, unless we've beaten a disease or sailed through a divorce, that we are boring. Nothing could be further from the truth.

Of course, we all want to listen to tales told by explorers and inventors. But we also can't relate to them. We can relate to the everyday experiences. But, we rarely think that our everyday experiences are interesting. The truth is, most of them aren't, although with an attitude of fascination, you can make virtually anything a great topic of conversation.

Here's how to make your life more interesting: because interest sparks interest, and that's the basis for great conversations.

Overcome Your Fears

"Inaction breeds doubt and fear. Action breeds confidence and courage. If you want to conquer fear, do not sit home and think about it. Go out and get busy."
~ Dale Carnegie

The biggest barrier to becoming more interesting is fear. We fear being judged and rejected. And so, we keep our true selves, our most wonderful ideas, safely buried inside. When we fear being seen as uninteresting, we become uninteresting.

Whenever you are operating out of fear, you automatically become less memorable, less attractive, and less charismatic. Why? Because fear shuts down your desire to *do* interesting things (things worth talking about). And then if you manage to do the things, you fear talking about them for fear of being judged.

Here's how to overcome the fear that makes you live a dull life.

Don't Be Lazy: Be in Action

"The best way to get something done is to begin." ~ Anonymous

Being interesting and being lazy do not go together: *ever*. You have to actually get out of the house and do something worthy of conversation. You do not have to go out and learn to be a helicopter pilot or learn to ride horses or take up trombone lessons just to have something interesting to talk about.

Action vaporizes fear! The more you *think* about something that intimidates you, the more afraid you become. If you just dive in… or dip your toe and take tiny steps… you will be more focused on what you are doing than on your fears.

Stepping out of your comfort zone just a little at a time, in baby steps, will help you broaden your horizons in comfortable ways.
- Travel, even if it's just for the weekend.
- Read something that expands your mind.
- Don't expect others to entertain you. Create your own amusement.

- Don't follow the herd. Do your own thing… the thing that makes your heart soar.

Challenge

Challenge yourself to learn something new every day.

Don't Do Uninteresting Things in Your Free Time

"I don't know where I'm going from here, but I promise it won't be boring." ~ David Bowie

What you do in your free time can be a source of endless conversation. What is not interesting? Sadly, it may be what you do in your free time.

- What you watched on Netflix that everybody else is watching: not interesting.
- You went out to eat at your favorite restaurant *again* this month: not interesting.
- You went to your favorite vacation spot again: not interesting.
- You eat the same 36 things regularly (it's a thing and most of us do this): not interesting.
- You scroll social media every day: not interesting.

What you can do instead, to become more interesting:

- Watch a documentary about a topic you are not really interested in. Today's documentaries are a far cry from the dry, factual documentaries of yesterday. Now, they are rich with color, emotion, experience… and just by expanding your mental horizons, you become more interesting.
- Try a new restaurant; and if you are dining at one of your favorite eateries, try a dish you haven't had before.

- Travel somewhere new, preferably as far out of your comfort zone as possible. Traveling in lands where you are completely unfamiliar with the language and the culture, broadens your horizons far more than travel to the same old places.
- Cook with one unfamiliar food each month, or more often if you are more adventurous.
- Ask a friend to join you on a photo safari in your favorite town or city. Even if neither of you is a photographer, just wandering around with your iPhone helps you see familiar things through the eyes of curiosity.

Don't stick to the default settings. Branch out and do interesting things. This will automatically give you topics of conversation that can help you learn more about others; and becoming more interested in others makes you more interesting.

Challenge

Make it a point to do one thing each month that you would normally not do, whether it's going to an art museum, reading a biography, going for a wilderness hike, volunteering at the animal shelter, etc. (as a bonus, you could meet fascinating people when you are out and about).

Don't Talk About Uninteresting Things

"It took me years to realize that 'normal' is actually super boring and that being myself was harder but infinitely more rewarding." ~ Franchesca Ramsey

Doing interesting things leads to being interesting but at the same time, again, if you make it about other people you instantly become more likable. You become more interesting when you are interested in the interesting things that other people do!

Don't:
- Ask boring questions like "What do you do?"
- Talk about TV shows.
- Talk about celebrities.
- Talk about the weather.

What's the point of boring conversation like this? Nothing! It doesn't make you likable: it makes you boring. You don't learn anything about the other person. They don't learn anything about you. The conversation becomes absolutely forgettable and meaningless.

And yet, so many people default to these topics because they are easy.

<u>Challenge</u>

Memorize some of the icebreakers in Chapter 7 (here we go again!) so you never have to default to talking about the weather. Food is always a great topic since it's one activity we all have in common.
- Ask them about the weirdest thing they have ever eaten.
- Ask them about the most challenging dish they have ever cooked that they are proud of.
- Ask them about their worst cooking disaster (like forgetting to put sugar in a cake).
- Ask them about the three best meals they have ever had.

Likable people will always turn the conversation around to you: what *you* like, what makes you tick, what lights you up inside. Fun and thought-provoking questions are the best way to get people talking about interesting things… and in the process, because you brought up an interesting topic, *you* will be perceived as more interesting.

Don't Fill Your Head with Fluff. Fill It with Interesting Things.

"I cannot remember the books I've read any more than the meals I have eaten; even so, they have made me." ~ Ralph Waldo Emerson

You have probably heard the saying, "You are what you eat." So true! But let's not forget that "You are what you drink, what you read, what you watch, and what you talk about." In other words, *you are what you consume.*

Boring people consume boring things:
- They get their news from one biased source (a source that confirms their beliefs), and never question what they see or try to understand a different perspective.
- They trust social media memes as a source of information.
- They only watch blockbuster movies that everyone is talking about.
- They only read best-selling books and gossip magazines.
- They eat fast food because it's easy, not because it's what their bodies need.

Yes, it's easier to follow along and do what everyone else is doing. But is it interesting? No! Instead:
- Get your news from less biased sources (you can Google which media companies lean conservative and which lean liberal, and choose news sources that are in the middle).
- For every news story you hear from your favorite source (which confirms your beliefs), watch a news story from a source with completely opposing views, so you can open your mind to their points of view.
- Do a "background check" on memes: get the facts, and then seek to understand the "why" of the person who posted the meme.

- Ask interesting people which movies made a lasting impact on them and watch those movies.
- Ask interesting people which books changed their lives and read them. In fact, fill your bookshelves with books that stimulate fascinating conversations (and be sure to read at least most of them, so that when people want to talk about your books, you don't have to stammer, "Uh, I haven't gotten to that one yet. Nope, not that one either.")

If you expect people to be interesting, they will often rise to the occasion: but it depends on the questions you ask them. Ask people about what intrigues them. Ask them what they recently learned. Ask them what beliefs they once held that they changed.

Challenge

Commit to uncovering some interesting tidbit about every person you meet because everyone has at least one interesting story to tell. Again, you do not want to interrogate them; but the icebreaker section in Chapter 7 is a great source of ideas.

Spend Time with Interesting People

"It's important to surround yourself with good people, interesting people, young people, young ideas. Go places, learn new stuff. Look at the world with wonder—don't be tired about it." ~ Angela Bassett

Have you noticed that many likable people hang out with people who are interesting? Did you ever wonder why?

It's because interesting people *explore each other.*

And that is why interesting people often hang out together. They encourage people around them to join them in doing interesting things. They talk about interesting topics and ideas and have meaningful conversations.

Surrounding yourself with interesting people can make you more likable because you learn how to be curious about other people!

"Curiosity creates connections." ~ Michelle Tillis Lederman

It's harder to learn to be interested in people who lead dull lives filled with mainstream entertainment and fast food. It's much more fun to hone your curiosity with interesting people; and to hang out with interesting people, you have to become one yourself (or, more accurately, you have to let your "interestingness" come out).

Challenge

Spend time this month with:
- The most well-traveled person you know
- The person who is the most fearless culinary adventurer you know
- The best conversationalist you know
- The most well-read person you know
- The person who knows the most about interesting movies/moviemakers (not celebrities)
- The weirdest person you know
- The funniest person you know
- The most adventurous person you know
- The most creative person you know
- The most scientific person you know

Prepare to have your mind opened! These people are by their very nature, fascinating. But you can apply the same conversation skills (asking interesting questions) to "ordinary people" who each have their own hidden, wonderful stories to tell.

Be Weird! Be Proud!

To other people, you are fascinating if you let your "weirdness" show. We are all weird, in our own delightful ways. We are the spice of life. Just imagine how boring life would be if everyone thought the same, talked the same, dressed the same, and did the same things. This is why it's important to:
- Be yourself, no matter how "weird" you are
- Be interested in others, and uncover their "weirdness"

On some level, we all fear losing our sense of self and becoming someone else just to fit in. Hopefully, throughout these chapters you have seen that this isn't the case. You can be you, in all your weirdness, and be very, very likable. Just remember to put your focus on the other person. Maybe you will find that you have some weirdness in common. Maybe you will discover a different kind of weirdness you didn't even know existed.

Never be ashamed of who you are because your "weirdness" is what makes you interesting. Be your weird, imperfect self. Set your values and stay true to yourself. Be proud of your individuality. Exploring your own "weirdness" can help you become more likable because you will be more curious about other people. And who doesn't love to talk about themselves and feel validated? The fact that you embrace your "weirdness" helps other people be themselves around you… and that is priceless.

People often hide themselves behind false facades because they are afraid of rejection. But they forget that they do not need acceptance from *everyone* in order to be happy and in order to forge amazing friendships.

There will always be the haters, the people who judge and criticize you, who are jealous of you, and who just don't like you. And that's okay.

All you need to find are the right people who embrace who you are. And when you aren't afraid to show yourself, it is easier to find such people.

"The truth is that we don't need everyone to like us; we need a few people to love us. Because what's better than being roundly liked is being fully known—an impossibility both professionally and personally if you are so busy being likable that you forget to be yourself." ~ Jessica Valenti

You can have quirks and weirdnesses that set you apart from the sort of bland and generic people who have chosen to hide who they are just to be liked.

You can act differently, dress differently, and talk differently and still be likable! As long as you are friendly and approachable, people will appreciate your uniqueness and the "spice" you bring to their lives.

Challenge

Have you ever found yourself trying to conform, just to fit in? This is a very common behavior in pre-teens and teenagers as they grow up and form social circles and learn social skills, but even adults do it. If you have ever done this, it is okay. You are not alone. However, if you are doing it now, challenge yourself to drop one of your conformist habits today.

For example, if you find yourself using a speech mannerism that you picked up from someone you admire, *challenge yourself to stop using it immediately*. Every time you are tempted to imitate someone, ask yourself if this is how you would be if nobody was watching.

Be yourself. Imitation may be the sincerest form of flattery… but is it *you*? No! People want to know *you*, not carbon copies of themselves. Even if you try to be just like someone, everybody will judge you for being an imitation.

Be the real thing. Do the one thing nobody else can do: be you.

Chapter 12: Putting It All Together

Likability Is a Skill: Practice Until You Embody It

"It's like everyone tells a story about themselves inside their own head. Always. All the time. That story makes you what you are. We build ourselves out of that story." ~ Patrick Rothfuss

Like any skill, likability is learned… and the rewards are earned. I hope that this book has boosted your confidence through the tips and tools I've shared.

Remember, take it slow. Don't try to apply all of these methods at once because when faced with overwhelm, the brain always wants to go back to its old ways: anytime there's a battle between something new and beliefs, beliefs usually win.

Beliefs like "Nobody likes me" die hard so the mental/emotional element of becoming a likable person is perhaps the most important part of this book.

Let's summarize the important points that will make you a likable person who makes friends easily and fosters the social connections that make for a rich, fulfilling, and meaningful life.

1. Likability does not mean being perfect, a people-pleaser, or a clone. It means you have developed several key traits, which can all be learned and practiced until they become second nature:
   - Kindness
   - A genuine interest in others
   - A positive and easygoing attitude
   - Empathy

- Passions (a fascination with life = fascination with people)
- Lack of ego
- A genuine desire to support others' dreams
- Good communication skills
- Being inclusive
- Emotional intimacy: sharing and keeping secrets
- Generosity and helpfulness
- Open-mindedness
- Open and friendly body language
- Self-awareness
- Vulnerability
- The ability to ask for help
- Restraint from giving unsolicited advice
- Seeing others as they want to be seen
- Emphasis on shared values
- Physical touch
- Cooperation and team spirit
- Natural leadership
- Ability to solicit opinions from everyone
- Being present and attentive
- Lack of complaining, judging, blaming, or criticizing
- Approachable and safe to talk to

2. Mindset: perhaps the most important skill to develop is a likable mindset, where you learn to undo your misconceptions of yourself as an unlikable person, and literally mentally rehearse yourself into being a friendly and wonderfully likable person. *If you believe you are likable, you will be!* This is the section that will require the most consistent practice and until you *believe* you are likable, the exercises in this book won't have as much impact.
- Upgrade your self-talk because for better or for worse, you become what you say you are.
- Take the 30-day likability mindset challenge to completely shake up who you "think" you are and mold yourself into a likable person.

- Mentally rehearse the ideal situation (you, surrounded by friends) with a powerful visualization exercise.
- Practice the way to say affirmations effectively for reprogramming yourself to BE a likable person.
- Use the feelings of gratitude and relief as the "push" that you need for successful self-reprogramming.
- Use the secret of repetition as a way to imprint a new way of thinking into your mind.

3. Make a good (and lasting) first impression by being relaxed using techniques such as holding a smile, the Power Pose, being punctual, presenting yourself well (for the "role" you want to play, not the one you are playing now), nonverbally communicating friendliness, immediately putting people at ease, being positive (attitude is everything), being present and not distracted, and maintaining personal space. And if all else fails and you've made a bad first impression, you can overcome it and forge a lasting relationship by "retraining" the other person to see you differently.

4. Create instant rapport using body language that is open and vulnerable (friendly): eye contact, a tall posture, open body position, stillness and relaxation, and your head position and facial expression. Physical touch and mirroring are two additional techniques that put people at ease.

5. Learning to master the art of conversation will spark interest and develop rapport. It is also necessary for developing a deep understanding of others: one of the key traits of likable people is that they are thirsty for knowledge about others! Use icebreakers to start a conversation and keep it going, restarting a stalled conversation, storytelling, muting yourself so you don't take over the conversation, talk about negative things without complaining, never gossip, and avoid
getting sucked into people's negativity.

6. Making people feel important in your eyes is vital to becoming a likable person. It involves being present and attentive, making it about them and not about yourself, non-judgmental validation, asking for more ("I'd love to hear more about…"), being genuinely complimentary, speaking kindly and respectfully about everyone, being empathetic, never talking down to someone, not offering unsolicited advice, using friendly phrases, becoming a great listener, building emotional intimacy, being open-minded, and finding common ground.

7. Acting like someone everybody wants to befriend is where it all comes together, building on the skills you learned. To sum up: always be kind, go with the flow, drop the ego, be inclusive, be generous and helpful (but know when to say no), be more self-aware, be warm and then competent, do what you need to do but ask for help when needed, and see others how they want to be seen.

8. Overcoming the likability bias in business is an important element of being successful while remaining likable: although this issue affects women much more than men, men should also understand what women are up against. Becoming an effective, respected, and a well-liked leader builds on the skills learned here.

9. All of the preceding skills lead up to one thing: allowing you to be yourself. First, you must overcome the fears that hold you back from presenting yourself to the world, by taking action, doing interesting things, talking about interesting things, learning interesting things, and surrounding yourself with interesting people so that you become naturally more curious about others… and therefore, more likable because you are showing interest. Above all, be proud of your "weirdness" because everybody is weird on some level; and the more interested you are in their weirdness, the more likable you become.

Likable, Wonderful You

As you can see, likability is a trait that is made up of many small elements that you can master one by one, step by step.

Don't put pressure on yourself to master everything quickly. A good place to start is to memorize some of the fun icebreakers outlined in Chapter 7, so you can get some small wins very quickly with an ability to approach someone and start up an interesting conversation.

And while you are working on the practical social skills, be sure to devote time and energy to developing your mindset.

You have probably heard the saying that true beauty comes from within. It's true! Being a likable person doesn't happen just from mastering the art of conversation or learning how to use body language to put someone at ease. Likability comes from within: a genuine curiosity about other people, and a genuine desire to be kind and helpful. But even before you turn your attention outward to focus on others, likability begins with liking yourself.

I encourage you to reread this book several times. There is a *lot* of information here to absorb! Most of all, be sure to do the challenges at the end of each section. You are working on up-leveling yourself through mental rehearsal as well as practical skills you can use in real situations with real people.

You will notice that if you commit to consistent practice, you will develop skills that genuinely likable people possess. And then, a whole new world will open up to you: a world of new friendships, opportunities, and chances to beautifully express yourself.

To your great success.